Patchwork
Embroidery

AIMEE RAY

Patchwork Embroidery

LARK

LARK

New York

An Imprint of Sterling Publishing Co., Inc.
1166 Avenue of the Americas
New York, NY 10036

ISBN 978-1-4547-0924-4

Distributed in Canada by Sterling Publishing Co., Inc.
c/o Canadian Manda Group, 664 Annette Street
Toronto, Ontario, Canada M6S 2C8
Distributed in the United Kingdom by GMC Distribution Services
Castle Place, 166 High Street, Lewes, East Sussex, England BN7 1XU

For information about custom editions, special sales, and premium and corporate purchases, please contact Sterling Special Sales at 800-805-5489 or specialsales@sterlingpublishing.com.

Manufactured in China

10 9 8 7 6 5 4 3 2 1

sterlingpublishing.com
larkcrafts.com

Design by Janet M. Evans-Scanlon
Photography by Cynthia Schaffer

Contents

Introduction

When you say patchwork, most people immediately think of quilts. Quilting is probably the most common way to use it, but literally and simply, patchwork is the act of sewing different pieces of fabric together to make any new fabric design. Patchwork fabric can then be stitched into anything you'd make with any other piece of fabric: bags, clothing, toys, artwork, housewares, and much more. Combine those endless possibilities with embroidery, and you've got ideas to keep your crafty heart and hands busy indefinitely.

I've always loved patchwork pieces. They are so full of colors, patterns, and life. There's something cozy about an item made from patched-together fabrics that makes you immediately think of the person who spent hours stitching all those little parts together. Heirloom pieces are particularly special and often treasured and handed down through families. The projects in this book will equip you to create your own heirlooms that will be treasured by generations to come.

I'm not really a quilter, so the projects I've designed are mostly simple squares or very freestyle patchwork, but thanks to the super-talented crafters I've enlisted to create even more sewing projects, you'll also find hexagons, English paper piecing, appliqué, and more. Together we've given you tons of patchwork inspiration and lots of fun techniques to try out. Each project includes specially designed embroidery embellishments to make it even more unique. Feel free to take the techniques you learn and use them to create your own unique designs!

I've also included more than a hundred new and original embroidery motifs to stitch on your projects. In the new motif library you'll find alternate patterns for most of the projects: mandalas, feathers, inspirational words, and a bunch of mini motifs perfect for stitching onto tiny hexagons or embellishing small projects. I've also scoured the Internet for vintage decor and sewing inspiration in order to create a special collection of vintage kitchen, sewing, and animal embroidery patterns inspired by the retro household kitsch we all love.

Have fun stitching!

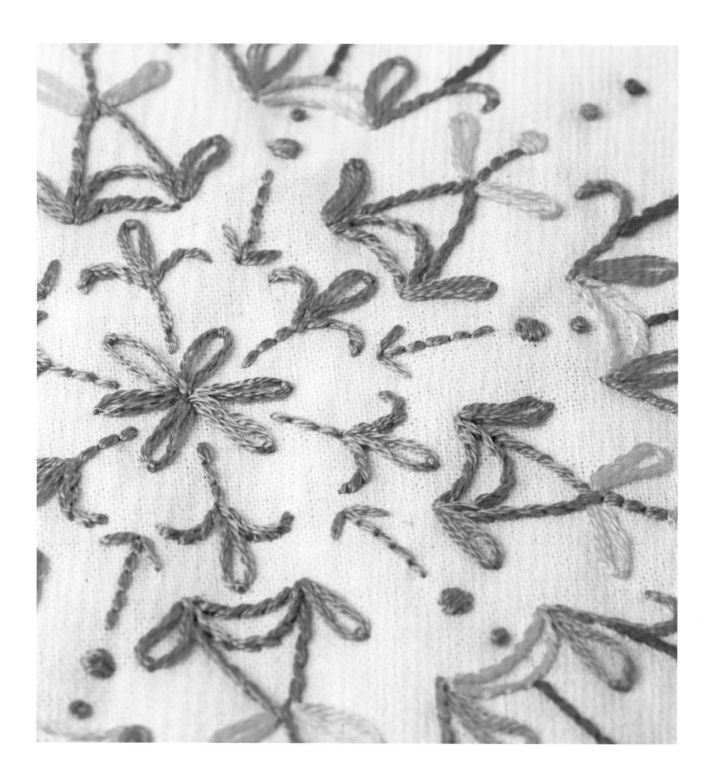

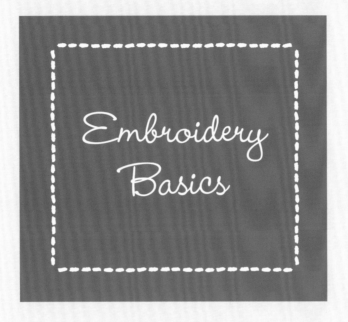

Embroidery Basics

I love that anyone can create something beautiful with just a needle, floss, a hoop, and some fabric. Of course, there are a few other items that will come in handy when embroidering and a few techniques to pick up along the way. But embroidery is one of the easiest crafts to learn, and doodle stitching is all about play and freedom—no need to count stitches or decipher confusing codes! This section of the book will teach you embroidery basics to get started, and the Sewing Essentials on page 18 will be handy for the projects that follow.

Materials & Tools

Floss

The variety of colors available for floss is truly astonishing. Floss is sold in small bundles, or *skeins*. Each strand of floss is made up of six threads, or *plies*, twisted together. For a thick embroidered line, use all six threads. For smaller, more delicate work, separate the threads and use fewer. I use either six or three threads for most embroidery projects. If I'm hand-sewing fabric together and using floss instead of sewing thread, I'll usually use one thread of floss.

Standard cotton floss is most common, but there are also many specialty flosses available, such as metallic, linen, silk, and gradient colors, which are fun to play with.

No one has ever accused me of being a neat freak, but I do love to organize. When my creative space and supplies are arranged so that I can easily see and find everything, I feel much more inspired to make things and use all the crafty stuff I've collected. There are lots of ways to organize your floss and lots of products on the market to help you.

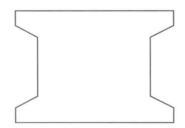

Each skein of embroidery floss comes wrapped with a paper band label showing the number designation of each color. When you unwrap a new skein of floss, keep track of that important number on the package. With hundreds of different floss colors, it's easy to forget the exact shade of aqua you were using. I can tell you from personal experience that it's frustrating to try to match colors from memory or that little length of floss in your purse. Instead, make it easy by winding your floss onto a cardboard bobbin and writing the number on the bobbin. The template I use to make mine is at the left.

I keep all my floss bobbins in a clear-plastic tackle box, arranged by color. I have one extra slot in the box for leftover floss pieces that are too long to throw away, and another for my scissors and a small pincushion with pins and needles. I can easily close the box up and put it away when I'm not using it (though usually it sits open on the couch in the living room, along with my current project) or even take it with me to use on the road.

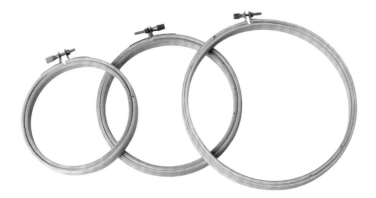

Needles

You don't really need a special type or size of needle for embroidering. All you need is one with a sharp point and a hole, or eye, that's large enough for you to thread floss through easily. Use a needle with a larger eye if you're using all six threads of floss, or use one with a small eye if you're using three or fewer threads or are hand-sewing with thread. I buy packs of several different sizes of needles so I have a variety to choose from. Keep a small pincushion close by so your needles won't get lost. You can easily make one of any shape or size by hand-sewing two pieces of felt together with a little stuffing inside. Don't forget to decorate it with embroidery!

Thimble

A thimble will make gripping and pushing the needle through a heavy or tightly woven fabric, such as canvas or denim, much easier on your fingers. Besides, you'll feel so domestic when you use one!

Embroidery Hoops

Although you can embroider some heavy, thick fabrics without a hoop, most fabrics will require one. Hooping your fabric will give you a tight, smooth surface to stitch on, and it will prevent puckering. Embroidery hoops consist of two round frames that fit together and tighten with a screw. The frames hold your fabric taut as you stitch. They come in plastic or wood and many different sizes. Plastic hoops are a good investment; they are sturdier than wood and will last a long time. You can use different-sized hoops for different-sized projects, but I've found a 6-inch (15.2 cm) one works well for almost anything.

EMBROIDERY TOOLBOX

Embroidery floss

Embroidery and sewing needles

Thimble

Embroidery hoop (a 6-inch [15.2 cm] circle is a good one to start with)

Sewing scissors

Fabric stabilizer

Tweezers

Straight pins

Nonpermanent fabric pen

Transfer or tracing materials and tools

Iron

Scissors

Any pair of scissors will do, but it's nice to have a small pair of sharp sewing scissors that you can keep with your embroidery floss and supplies.

Fabric and Other Materials

Here's my rule for fabric: If you can stick a needle through it, you can embroider it! The most common, and the fabric used for many of the projects in this book, is quilter's cotton. Felt, canvas, denim, and satin are also great fabrics to embroider on. Nothing is safe in my house when I have floss and needle in hand. Embroidery is such an easy way to add a personal touch to towels, pillowcases, curtains, sweaters, and sweatshirts.

And you don't need to stop at fabrics—I certainly don't. Heavy paper, vinyl, thin plastics, and even balsa wood can also be embroidered. To stitch on balsa wood, first apply a layer of white craft glue and a thin cotton fabric to the back to prevent cracking. When stitching on wood or paper, poke holes from the front first to come through from the back. It's best to stick with simpler stitches, and not to pull through so tightly that the paper rips or the balsa wood cracks. With a little extra care, you can make lots of unique projects with embroidery on these surfaces.

Stabilizer

Use a fabric stabilizer when embroidering on stretchy or delicate fabrics, such as T-shirt cotton or silk: It will keep the fabric from stretching as you work to help make a smoother finished product. Stabilizer comes in many varieties. The type I use most is the tear-away paper kind with an adhesive back. You can easily cut it to whatever size or shape you need, stick it onto the back of your fabric, and even remove and reposition it if necessary. You embroider right through the paper and fabric together. When you're done, just gently tear away the excess, and use tweezers or the tip of your needle to remove any bits of paper caught under the stitches. For delicate fabrics, I use a water-soluble stabilizer that easily dissolves in water once I'm done embroidering.

6

Transferring Patterns

Okay, transferring patterns is not the most enjoyable part of the process. But over the years, I've found several different methods to do so, depending on the different types of fabric I'm transferring the pattern to. Experiment with the methods that follow to find the best match for you and your fabric. (It's a good idea to test any fabric pens or iron-on prints on a piece of scrap fabric before using them on your actual project.)

Light Method

My old standby method is to trace patterns using a light table or a sunny window. I simply tape the pattern to a light table or window and secure the fabric over it so the pattern lines show through the fabric. My favorite tools for tracing pattern lines onto fabric are water-soluble fabric markers. Fabric-marker lines are easy to remove with water when you're done embroidering. An ordinary pencil will work, too; although it is more difficult to remove, so be sure to cover lead pencil lines completely with your embroidery. The light-table or sunny-window method works best for lightweight, light-colored fabrics.

Carbon Paper Method

Another way to transfer patterns to fabric is by using fabric carbon paper. You can find it in most fabric and craft stores. It comes in a variety of colors to contrast with the color of fabric you're using. Place your fabric on a hard surface, set a piece of carbon paper (carbon side down) on top of it, and your pattern on top of that. Trace the pattern lines with a pencil or other blunt object, such as a knitting needle. I use this method mostly for darker-colored fabrics that marker lines don't show up on.

Iron-On Transfers

A third method is to make an iron-on transfer. Just use a black-and-white laser print or photocopy of any design (unfortunately, prints from ink-jet printers won't work). Place the print on top of your fabric facedown, and iron it to transfer the image onto the fabric. Remember that you'll need to reverse the image before printing it, or it will be backward when you apply it to your fabric—this is especially important if your pattern includes text. The lines will be permanent, though they may fade with washing or over time, so you'll need to cover them completely with your embroidery. Homemade iron-on transfers can vary greatly depending on the type of paper, ink, and fabric you're using, so you may need to experiment a bit with this method.

Tissue Paper Method

One of my favorite transferring techniques (especially when working with thick fabrics like felt) is to trace the pattern onto thin, paperlike tissue or tracing paper, pin the paper to the fabric, and stitch right through the paper and the fabric together. When you're done, just tear away the paper. Use tweezers or the tip of your needle to remove any bits of paper caught under the stitches.

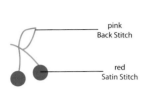

pink
Back Stitch

red
Satin Stitch

dark beige
French Knot

dark beige
Back Stitch

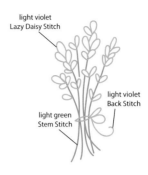

light violet
Lazy Daisy Stitch

light violet
Back Stitch

light green
Stem Stitch

Choosing & Using Motifs

This book includes motifs at the ends of individual projects and at the end of the book. You'll need to first trace the designs onto tracing paper or photocopy them. Some motifs will need to be enlarged by a specified percentage to fit the project size. Then transfer the motif to your fabric using one of the methods previously described. Remember, if you're using the iron-on transfer method, you'll need to reverse your images first so they don't end up backward on your fabric.

Keep in mind that the colors in the book and the stitches listed for the motifs used in the projects are just recommendations. If you lean toward red instead of pink, go for it. If you want to vary stitches to add extra details or textures that may not be included in the pattern, be my guest. I often improvise at the stitching stage, which is one reason I like to use removable fabric markers: That way, I'm free to change my mind as I work and can easily remove any pattern lines left over when I'm finished.

Get Stitching!

Okay, you've chosen your motifs, transferred your pattern to the fabric, and applied stabilizer (if needed)—now it's time to hoop your fabric. Simply place the fabric over the inside frame of an embroidery hoop and slip the outer frame on top, fitting them together. Tighten the screw, and gently pull the edges of the fabric until it's taut.

Next, choose a color of floss, cut a length about 12 inches (30.5 cm) long, and thread your needle. If it resists going through the needle's eye, try dampening one end of the floss and twisting it to a point. Tie a knot in the other end of the floss. One way to tie a knot is to wrap it around your finger, roll it off so that the thread twists around itself, and pull downward to tighten it.

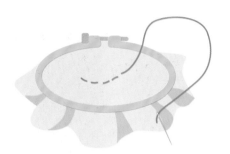

Now you are ready to start embroidering! Pull the needle and floss through from the back of your fabric until the knot catches. Choose a stitch and follow the pattern's lines. When you finish a line or color section of embroidery stitches, or you get down to about 2 inches (5.1 cm) of floss, tie a small knot on the back by slipping your needle under a stitch, looping it, and pulling it tight. Snip off the extra floss and start again.

You can work on your embroidery section by section, completing each area before moving onto the next one, or stitch a single color throughout the design before moving onto the next color.

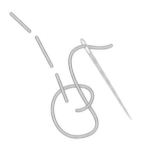

Watch Your Back

I'm not too fussy when embroidering on thick fabrics or making projects where the back of the embroidery will be hidden. However, you will want to keep the back of your embroidery neat if it will be visible, such as on a dish towel or on very thin, light-colored fabrics, where messy knots or tails of floss can show through the fabric. To keep the backs of your embroidery looking neat, tie knots tightly and close to the fabric and snip off any extra floss right above the knot. Also, limit the distance you stretch your floss across the back from stitch to stitch. Tie off your floss with each section of the design and start with a new knot at the next point, rather than stretching your floss from point to point. I usually don't stretch my floss longer than ½ inch (1.3 cm); this reduces the "spiderweb" effect on the back.

Finishing

When you've finished your embroidery, remove the fabric from the hoop and erase any removable transfer lines by rinsing it with water or hand-washing it with a gentle detergent. Press the water out by spreading the fabric flat or rolling it between two towels. When it's almost dry, lightly iron it facedown on a towel. This will remove any wrinkles but prevent crushing your stitches.

Stitch Library

Straight Stitch

The Straight Stitch is the most basic embroidery stitch. Just pull your needle through from the back at point A and push it back down at point B. Straight Stitches can be any length, from a tiny dot to a line about ¼ inch (6 mm) long. Make several Straight Stitches in a line to form the Running Stitch, or position them in a circle, starting each stitch at the center and ending pointed outward, to make a flower shape. You can also stitch them individually or in groupings for small details like eyes or fur.

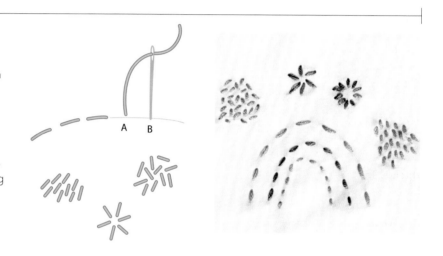

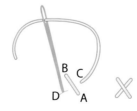

Cross Stitch

Start with a small diagonal Straight Stitch, from A to B. Make a second stitch over it from C to D. Rows of Cross Stitches look neater when the lines for each cross overlap in the same direction. If you're making a row, you can stitch a line of identical diagonal stitches, then go back and cross over them in the other direction.

Star Stitch

Stars can be made in the same way as Cross Stitches. Start by making a Cross Stitch, and then add an additional Straight Stitch on top of it, from A to B.

Another way to make a Star is by making several Straight Stitches in a circle, ending at the same center point. Make your first stitch from A to B, your second stitch from C to B, and so on. Continue around the center, adding as many stitches as you like until you reach the first stitch.

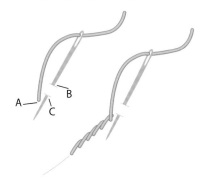

Split Stitch

Split Stitch lines are quick and easy to make and make great outlines.

Make a small Straight Stitch from A to B. Bring the needle back up at C, splitting the first stitch in half. Continue making stitches and splitting them to form a line.

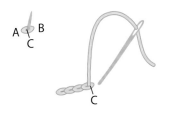

Stem Stitch

The Stem Stitch is perfect for stitching curved lines or flower stems, which is how it got its name. Make a stitch from A to B, leaving the floss a little loose. Pull the needle to the front again at C, between A and B and just to one side. Pull the floss tight and continue to form a line of stitches.

Back Stitch

The Back Stitch is a nice, clean outlining stitch. Start with a small stitch in the opposite direction, from A to B. Bring your needle back through the fabric at C, ahead of the first stitch and ending at A. Repeat to make each new Back Stitch, working backward on the surface and inserting the needle at the end of the previous stitch.

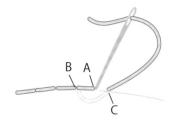

Chain Stitch

The Chain Stitch is great for a thick outline but also works nicely as a decorative border. Pull the needle and floss through the fabric at A (figure 1). Insert the needle back in at A, pulling the floss through to the back until you have a small loop on the front. Bring the needle back up through the fabric inside of the loop at B (figure 2). Reinsert the needle at B, pulling the floss through to form a second small loop. Continue stitching loops to make a Chain (figure 3). When you finish a row, make a tiny stitch over the end of the last loop to hold it in place.

To end a Chain Stitch circle, stop one stitch short of the first stitch, and slide your needle and floss underneath it at C (figure 4). Then finish the last stitch, completing the circle.

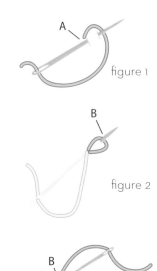

figure 1

figure 2

figure 3

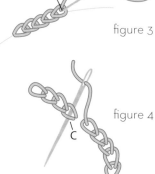

figure 4

Blanket Stitch

The Blanket Stitch makes a great decorative border or edging. Make a loose, diagonal stitch from A to B. Bring the needle up again at C, catching the floss under the needle and pulling it tight to the fabric.

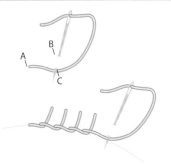

French Knot

French Knots can be tricky at first, but they are well worth taking the time to learn. Individually, they make great dot accents or fill an area solidly with French Knots for an interesting texture. Bring the needle through the fabric at A. Wrap the floss around the tip of the needle in the direction shown, and reinsert the needle at B, right next to A. Pull the floss tight and close to the fabric as you pull the needle back through. You can make larger French Knots by wrapping the floss around the needle multiple times.

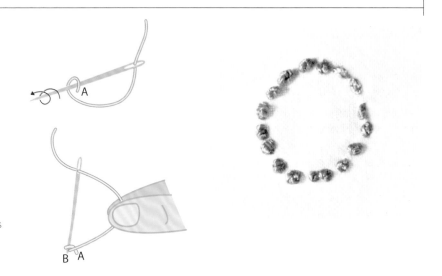

Lazy Daisy Stitch

The Lazy Daisy Stitch is the perfect way to make flower petals and leaves. You can use Satin Stitches or French Knots to make the flower centers. Bring your needle through the fabric at A and put it back down in the same spot, but don't pull the floss all the way through; leave a small loop. Now bring your needle back through the fabric inside the loop at B and back down at C, catching the loop at the top and securing it to the fabric. Repeat this stitch in a circle to make a daisy.

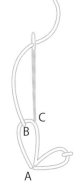

Fly Stitch

The Fly Stitch is an interesting decorative accent stitch. Make a loose horizontal stitch from A to B. Press the loop flat to one side with your finger. Bring the needle back up at C, in the center of the first stitch. Return the needle at D, securing the first stitch to the fabric.

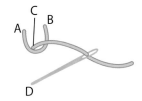

Scallop Stitch

The Scallop Stitch is a cousin to the Fly Stitch and Lazy Daisy Stitch and is made with the same basic technique. Scallop Stitches are great for making flowers or leaves. Stitch several in a row to make a pretty border. Make a loose stitch from A to B, and press it flat to one side with your finger. Bring the needle to the front of the fabric at C, inside the loop. Insert the needle at the outside of the stitch, at D, to hold it in place.

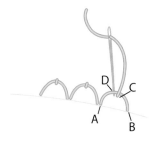

Satin Stitch

Satin Stitches are a lovely way to fill in small areas with smooth, solid color. Make a Straight Stitch from A to B. Make a second stitch right next to the first one from C to D. Always bring your needle up on one side and down on the other for best results. If you have trouble keeping the edges of your area even, first outline the shape with a tight Back Stitch or Split Stitch, and make your Satin Stitches over the top. For an extra-smooth area of Satin Stitches, untwist and separate the threads of floss first.

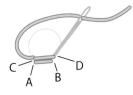

Long and Short Stitch

The Long and Short Stitch is used to cover large areas with solid or blended color. Start the first row by making a stitch from A to B. Next, make another stitch right next to it from C to D, only half as long. Repeat making a long stitch, then a short one to form the first row. Only the first row has both long and short stitches, the rest of the stitches will all be the same length. For the second row, make stitches just below your first row of stitches, filling in the spaces. Unless you're stitching a perfect square of Long and Short Stitches, they probably won't all be perfectly uniform, and that is just fine. Add a stitch here and there to fill in any gaps as you go along. Just keep your stitches all going in the same direction, and you'll have an evenly filled area when you're finished.

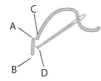

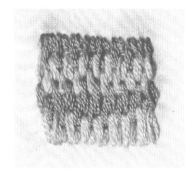

Sewing Essentials

Appliqué

Stitching a piece of contrasting colored or patterned fabric onto your embroidery fabric surface adds color and interest to your work.

Felt is a great fabric to use for appliqués. It is thick and easy to cut, and the edges don't fray. For a felt appliqué, just cut out the finished shape and stitch it onto the background fabric.

When using cotton or other fabric for appliqués, you can either use pinking shears for a decorative edge, or you can fold the edges under. Felt shapes or other fabric shapes cut with pinking shears can be added using any embroidery stitch or the Appliqué Stitch.

To hide fraying fabric edges, draw your shape onto the fabric and cut it out, but leave ¼-inch (6.4 mm) seam to the back of the appliqué shape and stitch it on with the Appliqué Stitch.

Another technique especially good for shapes with curved edges is to cut a second piece of fabric in the same shape as your appliqué piece. Sew them together with right sides facing, leaving a 1-inch (2.5 cm) opening. Notch the edges, turn the piece right side out, and press it flat.

Now the edges are neatly hidden, and you can stitch the appliqué onto your fabric. You can even stuff the piece for a three-dimensional effect or cut away the hidden fabric behind the appliqué if you want it flatter.

Appliqué Stitch

Pin the appliqué shape in place on the fabric background. Pull a knotted length of thread from the back of the background fabric to the front at A, very near the edge, and through the appliqué. Insert the needle back through the background fabric at B, and bring the tip of the needle up again at C. Pull the thread tightly through, securing the fabrics together. Continue making even, equally spaced stitches around the perimeter of the appliqué.

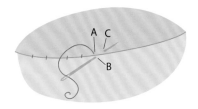

Basting Stitch

The Basting Stitch is used to hold a seam in place until you sew it permanently. It is just a long, loose Straight or Running Stitch. Knot your thread and stitch around the seam. When you've sewn it in place, pull out the basting thread.

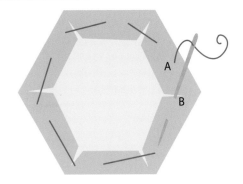

Hidden Stitch

A few of the projects in this book are sewn inside out, turned right side out through an unstitched opening called the *turning gap*, and then stuffed. The Hidden Stitch is a nearly invisible stitch you can use to close the opening. To do so, first fold the excess fabric in along each side of the opening and pin the hole closed. Prepare a needle with thread matching the color of the fabric and knot it at one end. Bring the needle and thread through the fabric from the back at A and back down directly across the opening at B. Slide the needle along the inside of the fold and pull it back out at C, trapping the stitch inside. Reinsert the needle across from C at D, pulling the thread tightly. Continue stitching along the opening, closing up the seam. When you get to the end, make a tiny knot buried in the seam.

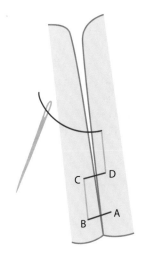

Slip Stitch

If you don't want your stitches to show when joining a hemmed or folded edge to a flat piece, the Slip Stitch is the way to go. It's useful for attaching bindings to quilts but also works well for closing the gap in a stuffed project. Begin by inserting your threaded needle through the fabric from the inside of a folded or hemmed edge, anchoring the knot inside the fabric. Insert the needle into the adjacent fabric just enough to pick up a few threads, then run the needle back down inside the top fold of the fabric.

Moving the needle point inside the fold the length of one stitch, bring it up through the top of the fold, pick up a few threads from the adjacent fabric, and push the needle back down through the top of the fold. Repeat until the edge is complete. Finish by burying a knot into the joined edge and then running the needle and remaining thread back inside the fold a short distance. Push the needle back through the top of the fold and trim the excess thread, leaving the tail hidden within the fold.

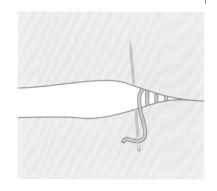

Stab Stitch

The Stab Stitch is a variation of the Running Stitch using very tiny stitches. It's most often used to attach a piece of fabric to a background fabric. Use thread matching the fabric

or one thread from a strand of floss. Bring the needle up at A and down at B, 1/8 inch (3 mm) from the edge of the fabric. Continue stitching all around the edge.

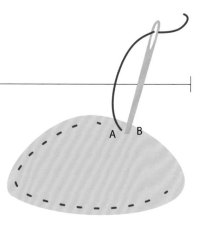

Topstitch

Topstitching is done by hand or machine after fabric pieces are sewn together and the project is turned right side out. Just sew a line of small

Straight Stitches close together through both layers of fabric. Topstitching is usually done close to and parallel with an edge.

Whip Stitch

Whip Stitches are a great way to add a decorative touch while joining pieces of fabric together. You can use Whip Stitches along matched edges or as an Appliqué Stitch, sewing one piece of fabric to another background piece. You can also use it to hem the raw edge of a piece of fabric or alone as a decorative stitch. Use matching thread to hide

your stitches or embroidery floss in a contrasting color to show them off.

Starting at the back or between two pieces of fabric, bring your needle and floss through at A. Bring the needle over the edge of the fabric (or through the background piece) and reinsert it from the back at B.

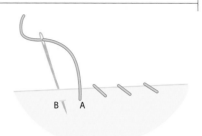

Notching Edges and Trimming Corners

When making projects such as pillows or stuffed pieces, you will sew two pieces of fabric together with the right sides facing. Before you turn the fabric pieces right side out again, you will want to first *notch* the fabric around the seam so that the edges of your finished project look neat and smooth.

For curved edges, cut small, triangular pieces out of the fabric, cutting right up to, but not through, your stitched seam (figure 1). Make notches ½ to 1 inch (1.3 to 2.5 cm) apart. The tighter the curve, the more notches should be cut. Cut corners off straight across as shown (figure 2).

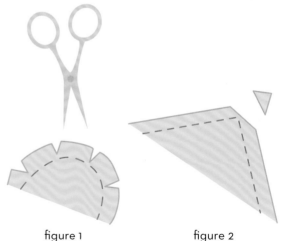

figure 1   figure 2

Projects

Animal Baby Book

PROJECT DESIGNER

Teresa Mairal Barreu

This book uses a typical layout with one rectangle making up two pages. The finished book size is 7 inches (17.8 cm) square. The colors I chose for the book are based on the blue Australian sky (the bluest sky in the world, they say), yellow for the sun, and orange for the red earth, which is very typical of Australia.

What You Need

EMBROIDERY THREAD

1 skein each of dark sandy brown, dark blue, topaz, dark beige, ombre brown tones, ombré gray tones, very light plum, and dark emerald green

BOOK COVERS

Motifs: Lettering and bilby (page 27)

1 square of cotton fabric, 7 × 7 inches (17.8 × 17.8 cm), embroidered

1 square of cotton fabric, 6 × 6 inches (15.2 × 15.2 cm), embroidered

Transfer paper

Iron

Towel

For the front cover: 1 quilt block, 9 patch pattern with an oversized center square (see instructions below)

> 4 rectangles of yellow cotton fabric, 5¾ × 1⅜ inches (14.6 × 3.5 cm)
>
> 4 squares of blue cotton fabric, 1⅜ × 1⅜ inches (3.5 × 3.5 cm)

For the back cover: 1 quilt block, shoo fly pattern (see instructions below)

> 4 strips of dark brown cotton fabric, 4½ × 2 inches (11.4 × 5.1 cm)
>
> 1 square of cotton fabric in blue polka dots, 3⅝ × 3⅝ inches (9.2 × 9.2 cm)
>
> 1 square of cotton fabric in dark brown, 3⅝ × 3⅝ inches (9.2 × 9.2 cm)

(continued on the following page)

Stitches

Book title: Stem Stitch in dark sandy brown for *Animals* lettering; Stem Stitch in dark blue for *Australian* lettering

Wombat: Stem Stitch in topaz for lettering; Back Stitch in dark beige for outline

Echidna: Back Stitch in ombré brown tones for spikes: Stem Stitch in dark beige for nose; Stem Stitch in dark blue for lettering

Emu: Back Stitch in topaz for wings and interior outlines; Satin Stitch in topaz for eye; Back Stitch in dark beige for legs; Stem Stitch in dark blue for lettering

Kangaroo: Running Stitch in dark beige for outside outline; Back Stitch in dark beige for inside outlines; Stem Stitch in dark blue for lettering

(continued on the following page)

(continued from the previous page)

Koala: Back Stitch in dark beige for outline; Stem Stitch in dark blue for lettering

Platypus: Running Stitch in dark beige for outside outline and lettering; Back Stitch in dark beige for inside outlines

Bilby: Stem Stitch in ombré gray tones and very light plum for outline; Stem Stitch in dark sandy brown for lettering

Eucalyptus leaf bookmark: Running Stitch in dark emerald green for outlining leaf contour; Back Stitch in dark emerald green for central vein

(continued from the previous page)

For the spine:

　　1 strip of black-and-white fabric, 1⅛ x 7½ inches

ANIMAL PAGES

Motifs: wombat, platypus, emu, kangaroo, koala, echidna, and lettering (page 27)

3 rectangles of cotton fabrics that have blue, yellow, and orange tones, 16 inch × 8 inch (40.6 × 20.3 cm)

Double-sided, iron-on transfer paper

Scraps of felt and fabrics in tan, dark gray, white, light gray, dark brown, and black

BOOKMARK

Motifs: leaf (page 27)

Green felt

Ribbon, 10 inches (25.4 cm) long

Straight pins

ASSEMBLING THE BOOK

2 pieces of batting or flannel, 15 × 7½ inches (38.1 × 19.1 cm)

Instructions

PRINTING DESIGN MOTIFS

1　Size the design motifs for the wombat at 175% of original, the platypus at 200%, the emu at 150%, the kangaroo at 135%, the koala at 200%, echidna at 190%, the bilby at 135%, and the leaf at 165%.

Australian Animals

Koala
- dark blue — Stem Stitch
- dark sandy brown — Stem Stitch
- dark beige — French Knot
- dark beige — Back Stitch
- dark blue — Stem Stitch

Platypus
- dark beige — Running Stitch
- dark beige — French Knot
- dark beige — Back Stitch
- dark beige — Running Stitch

Wombat
- dark beige — French Knot
- dark beige — Back Stitch
- topaz — Stem Stitch

Kangaroo
- dark beige — Back Stitch
- dark beige — French Knot
- dark beige — Running Stitch
- dark beige — Running Stitch
- dark blue — Stem Stitch

Emu
- topaz — Satin Stitch
- topaz — Back Stitch
- dark beige — Back Stitch
- dark blue — Stem Stitch

leaf
- dark emerald green — Back Stitch
- dark emerald green — Running Stitch

echidna
- ombré brown tones — Back Stitch
- dark beige — French Knot
- dark beige — Stem Stitch
- dark blue — Stem Stitch

bilby
- very light plum — Stem Stitch
- ombré gray tones — French Knot
- ombré gray tones — Stem Stitch
- very light plum — Stem Stitch
- dark sandy brown — Stem Stitch

27

BOOK COVERS EMBROIDERED SQUARES

1 Cut a 7-inch (17.8 cm) square for the front cover and a 6-inch (15.2 cm) square for the back cover.

2 Transfer the title design onto the 7-inch (17.8 cm) square and the bilby design onto the 6-inch (15.2 cm) square.

3 Embroider using the colors and stitches shown in the designs on page 27.

4 Trim the title square to 5¾ inches (14.6 cm) and the bilby square to 4½ inches (11.4 cm) after embroidering.

FRONT COVER QUILT BLOCK (9 PATCH PATTERN)

1 Cut 4 yellow rectangles, 5¾ × 1⅜ inches (14.6 × 3.5 cm), and 4 blue squares, 1⅜ inches (3.5 cm).

2 Take one yellow rectangle and sew one blue square to each end.

3 Repeat with a second yellow rectangle and the 2 remaining blue squares.

4 Sew 1 yellow rectangle to one side of the embroidered title square and the other yellow rectangle to the opposite side of the title square.

5 Sew 2 completed yellow and blue strips to the other 2 sides of the embroidered title square.

BACK COVER QUILT BLOCK (SHOO FLY PATTERN)

1   Cut 4 strips of fabric in dark brown, 4½ × 2 inches (11.4 × 5.1 cm).

2   To make the half square triangle (HST) corners, cut one square of fabric in blue polka dots, 3⅝ inches (9.2 cm), and another square of fabric in dark brown, 3⅝ inches (9.2 cm).

3   Place both squares with wrong sides facing together, and sew all around the edges, leaving ¼-inch (6 mm) seam allowance.

4   Cut along one diagonal and then along the other diagonal. This results in 4 half square triangles (HSTs).

5   Unfold each HST, and press the seam open to flatten to the piece into a square.

6   Match the dark brown edges of 2 of the HSTs to the ends of one of the 4½ × 2-inch (11.4 × 5.1 cm) strips of dark brown fabric, using the photo on page 28 as a guide. Sew the HSTs to the strip.

7   Repeat step 6 with the remaining 2 HSTs and a second strip of dark brown fabric.

8   Sew 2 dark brown strips to the top and bottom of the embroidered bilby square.

9   Next sew 1 completed strip to each side of the embroidered bilby square, completing a brown border around the embroidered square.

10 To join the front and back cover blocks together, make the spine of the book by cutting a strip of black-and-white striped fabric, 1⅛ × 7½ inches (2.9 × 19.1 cm).

11 Place the front cover block faceup, and align the spine fabric facedown (right sides together) on top of and along the left edge of the cover, making sure to align the tops and bottoms. Pin the edges together to hold them in place, and sew along the edge, leaving ¼-inch (6 mm) seam allowance.

12 Open the joined spine and front cover piece, and place it faceup with the spine on the left and the bottom nearest to you. Align the back cover on top of and facedown (right sides together) along the spine edge with the bottom nearest to you. Be sure to align the top and bottom edges neatly. Make certain that the words on each panel are oriented in the same direction. Pin the edges together to hold them in place, and sew along the edge, leaving ¼-inch (6 mm) seam allowance.

ANIMAL PAGES

1   Cut 3 rectangles from different fabrics that have blue, yellow, and orange tones, 16 × 8 inches (40.6 × 20.3 cm).

2   Draw a vertical line down the middle at the 8-inch mark (20.3 cm) to make 2 pages per rectangle.

3   Size animal designs to sizes indicated on page 26. Then trace *only the outlines* of the wombat, emu body, kangaroo, koala, and platypus designs onto the double-sided iron-on transfer paper. These pieces will be ironed to fabrics. When using double-sided iron-on transfer paper, if you trace the designs on the paper side, the designs will be reversed. You can print the designs reversed, or you can trace on the side that has the glue to keep the original image.

4   Cut loosely around the drawn shapes.

5   Place the iron-on transfer paper on the wrong side of the fabric you have chosen for each animal, and press following the manufacturer's instructions.

6   Cut out the design along the drawn lines.

7   Peel off the transfer paper.

8   Now take one of the book page rectangles and center the design on one of the pages. Note: Each rectangle will have 2 animals, and both need to be centered on each side.

9 Press with your iron to adhere the design.

10 Continue transferring the rest of the design onto the fabric using the best method of transfer for the fabrics you are using.

11 Position each animal's name template beneath its image and transfer it onto the fabric.

12 As you work through each page of the book, embellish the appropriate animal with the following additional features. These shapes should be traced onto double-sided iron-on transfer paper and ironed to felt or fabric as indicated.

- Head of joey in tan felt
- Joey's pouch in a darker fabric
- Koala's nose in black felt
- Tummy of koala in a white fabric
- Beak and paws of platypus in dark brown felt
- Wombat nose in dark brown felt

13 Cut out the animal features along the design lines. Position each piece on the animal and iron in place according to the manufacturer's instructions.

14 As this is a baby book, it is important that all the shapes are well secured. With a matching color thread, stitch very close to the edge along all shapes that have been bonded to the pages.

15 Embellish each shape with embroidery.

16 Once all the animals are finished, trim all pages to 7½ × 15 inches (19 × 38 cm).

BOOKMARK

1 Size the leaf design as indicated on page 26. Then trace the design onto a piece of felt that has been folded in half, and cut 2 leaves at the same time.

2 Cut a piece of ribbon 10 inches (25.4 cm) long and place it in between the leaves, running it centered down the length of the leaf (see the photo below). Pin in place, and use a Back Stitch to create the central vein of the leaf and to anchor the ribbon securely inside the leaf.

3 Using a Running Stitch, embroider around the contour of the leaf (see the photo below).

ASSEMBLING THE BOOK

1 Cut 2 pieces of thin batting or flannel that are 7½ × 15 inches (19 × 38 cm).

2 Place the cover and page one together with the right sides facing each other. Ensure that the words are facing in the same direction. Place the bookmark in between the pages, aligning it over the book's spine. Align the ribbon edge with the top edge of the rectangle (the edge opposite to the animal name). Then place the batting on top of the wrong side of the first rectangle.

3 Sew around the edges, leaving ¼-inch (6 mm) seam allowance and a 3-inch (7.6 cm) opening to turn the pages right side out.

4 Turn the pages right side out, taking care to gently pull the bookmark out without detaching it from the pages.

5 Repeat with rectangles 2 and 3. Place rectangle 2 right side up, then rectangle 3 right side down, making sure the words on both rectangles are facing in the same direction. Next, place the batting on top, and sew all three layers together, leaving a 3-inch (7.6 cm) opening to turn the piece right side out.

6 Turn the rectangle right side out.

7 To close the openings, use a Hidden Stitch or similar invisible stitch.

8 Press pages well.

9 Place the rectangles in the correct order, cover facing down first, words in the right direction, then rectangle 2, and then rectangle 3 on top.

10 Pin well in the middle to hold all pages together. Stitch through the spine of the book.

Feather Arrow Backpack

PROJECT DESIGNER

AIMEE RAY

Satin Stitches on frayed edge appliqué add a unique, rugged look to this backpack.

What You Need

Templates: arrow and feather (page 151)

1 piece of tan or tea-dyed twill fabric, 10 × 6 inches (25.4 × 15.2 cm)

Embroidery floss, one skein each of light brown, brown, dark brown, aqua, gray, and ecru

Brown canvas backpack with a 10-inch (25.4 cm) wide flap

Iron-on adhesive hem tape

Stitches

Stem Stitch, Satin Stitch, Straight Stitch

Instructions

1 Size the feathers and arrow templates to the size indicated on page 151. Then trace the feather and arrow templates onto the twill and embroider the designs according to the patterns.

2 Cut out the pieces, leaving ¼ inch (6 mm) extra around the template lines. Fray the edges of the fabric up to the template line by pulling them through your forefinger and thumbnail.

3 Arrange the embroidered pieces onto the flap of the backpack and iron them on with strips of hem tape behind each one. Use a small amount of hem tape behind each piece, enough to cover the feather but not overlapping the fringe.

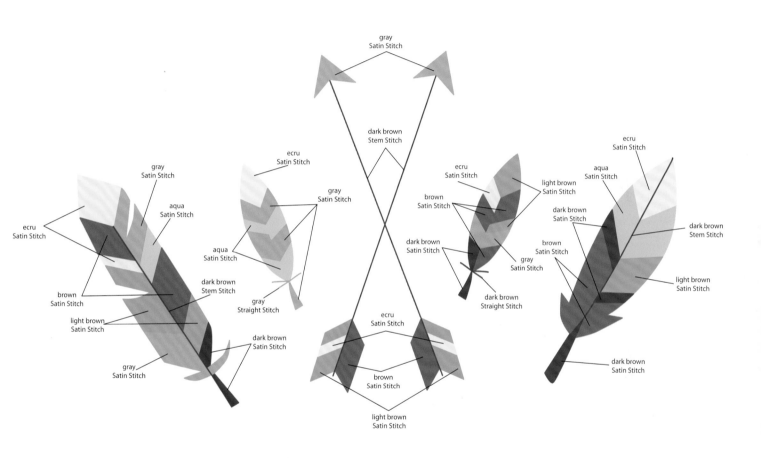

gray
Satin Stitch

dark brown
Stem Stitch

gray
Satin Stitch

aqua
Satin Stitch

ecru
Satin Stitch

ecru
Satin Stitch

ecru
Satin Stitch

light brown
Satin Stitch

aqua
Satin Stitch

ecru
Satin Stitch

aqua
Satin Stitch

gray
Satin Stitch

brown
Satin Stitch

dark brown
Satin Stitch

ecru
Satin Stitch

brown
Satin Stitch

dark brown
Stem Stitch

dark brown
Stem Stitch

brown
Satin Stitch

light brown
Satin Stitch

dark brown
Satin Stitch

brown
Satin Stitch

dark brown
Satin Stitch

light brown
Satin Stitch

gray
Satin Stitch

dark brown
Satin Stitch

gray
Straight Stitch

gray
Satin Stitch

dark brown
Straight Stitch

light brown
Satin Stitch

brown
Satin Stitch

dark brown
Satin Stitch

light brown
Satin Stitch

Camper Zipper Pouch

PROJECT DESIGNER

CYNTHIA SHAFFER

What You Need

Camper Zipper Pouch templates A-H (page 153)

White cotton fabric for the front of the camper pouch, 10 × 8 inches (25.4 × 20.3 cm)

White cotton fabric for the lining of the front of the camper pouch, 10 × 8 inches (25.4 × 20.3 cm)

Disappearing fabric marker

Scraps of cotton fabric in turquoise, black, gray/white striped, and lime green for the camper

Fusible web, 6 × 6 inches (15.2 × 15.2 cm)

Embroidery floss in gray, green, pink, red, and yellow

Scraps of printed cotton fabric in pink, fuchsia, green, and turquoise

Green fabric that measures 11 × 8 inches (27.9 × 20.3 cm)

Blue zipper, 9 inch (22.8 cm)

Turquoise fabric that measures 10 × 10 inches (25.4 × 25.4 cm)

Temporary fabric spray adhesive

Stitches

Back Stitch, Satin Stitch, Lazy Daisy Stitch, French Knot

Instructions

NOTE: *Seam allowance is ¼ inch (6 mm) throughout.*

FRONT PANEL

1   Size template A as shown on page 153. Copy it onto a sheet of copy paper, and then cut out around the shape.

2   Layer the 2 pieces of white cotton fabric on top of each other, and pin template A onto the fabric. Cut out the shape. Using a lightbox, transfer all the camper markings and fabric placements onto one piece of fabric with a disappearing fabric marker.

3   Using spray adhesive, adhere the two pieces of white fabric together.

    NOTE: *As an alternative to using spray adhesive, you can layer the white fabrics and stitch around the pieces, close to the outer edge.*

4   Size templates B-H as shown on page 153. Copy them onto copy paper, and cut out around the shapes. Place the shapes onto the paper side of the fusible web, and trace around the shapes, leaving 1 inch (2.5 cm) between. Cut out around the shapes about ½ inch (1.3 cm) outside the traced lines.

5   Place the web side of the traced shapes onto the wrong side of the scraps of fabric. Place B and C onto turquoise fabric, D and E onto black fabric, F and G onto gray/white striped fabric, and H onto green fabric. Following the manufacturer's directions, fuse the shapes to the fabric.

6   Cut out the fused shapes along the traced lines, and then peel off the paper backing.

7   Position the pieces on the white camper fabric according to the design markings and, following the manufacturer's directions, fuse the fabric pieces in place.

    NOTE: *Template F will be fused on top of template D.*

8   Using a Back Stitch with gray embroidery floss, embroider around all the pieces and around the camper shape. Using a Satin Stitch with green embroidery floss, embroider the stool. Using a Satin Stitch with alternating pink, red, and yellow embroidery floss, embroider the banner flags and the heart. Using a Lazy Daisy Stitch with alternating pink and red embroidery floss, embroider the flowers. Embroider red French Knots at the center of the flowers.

9   Using the scraps of cotton fabrics, cut out the patchwork pieces for the front, bottom, and the sides of the pouch: For the front, cut 3 pieces that measure 2¼ × 2 inches (5.8 × 5.1 cm) and 4 pieces that measure 2¼ × 1¼ inches (5.8 × 3.2 cm). For the sides, cut 2 pieces that measure 2¼ × 2 inches (5.8 × 5.1 cm) and 8 pieces that measure 2¼ × 1¼ inches (5.8 × 3.2 cm).

FRONT BOTTOM PATCHWORK

1   With the right sides facing each other, sew together 2 of the 2¼ × 1¼ pieces (5.8 × 3.2 cm) along the longest side. Make another piece just like this one.

2   With right sides facing each other, sew together one of the 2¼ × 2 pieces (5.8 × 5.1 cm) with one of the segments made in step 7 along the short ends. Stitch this piece to another 2¼ × 2 inches (5.8 × 5.1 cm) piece (right sides together and short end to short end), and then sew the other segment made in step 1. To the end, stitch the last piece that measures 2¼ × 2 inches (5.8 × 5.1 cm). Press the seams to one side.

3   With right sides facing, sew this patchwork strip to the bottom of the camper front. Press the seam toward the patchwork strip.

PATCHWORK SIDES

1   Using the scraps of cotton fabrics, cut out 2 pieces that measure 2¼ × 2 inches (5.8 × 5.1 cm) and 8 pieces that measure 2¼ × 1 ¼ inches (5.8 × 3.2 cm).

2   With right sides facing each other, sew together 2 of the 2¼ × 1 ¼ (5.8 × 3.2 cm) pieces along the longest side. Make 3 more pieces just like this one.

3   With right sides together, sew one of the segments made in step 2 with one of the 2¼ × 2 inches (5.8 × 5.1 cm) pieces along the short ends, and then add on another one of the pieces made in step 2. This is one of the pouch sides. Make a second patchwork segment like this for the other side of the pouch. Press the seam allowance to the side.

ZIPPER OPENING

1   From the green fabric, cut 2 strips that measure 10 × 1 inches (25.4 × 2.5 cm).

2   With right sides facing, pin and then sew 1 green strip to the outer edge of one side of the zipper. Repeat for the other side.

NOTE: *The 10-inch (25.4 cm) strip will extend about ¼ inch (6 mm) past the zipper stop at both ends. Trim away any excess zipper fabric that extends beyond the green fabric.*

3 With right sides facing each other, sew one of the side patchwork pieces to each end of the zipper section. Press the seam allowance away from the zipper. Topstitch close to the seam all the way around the zipper.

BACK PANEL

1 Place the pouch front onto the turquoise fabric and pin in place. Cut around the camper front to create the back panel.

POUCH BOTTOM

1 Cut out 1 piece from the green fabric that measures 9 × 2 inches (22.8 × 5.1 cm).

ASSEMBLING THE POUCH

1 Place the pouch faceup. Position the green bottom facedown (right sides together) along the bottom edge of the pouch back. Sew the green panel to the pouch back along the bottom edge. Start stitching ¼ inch (6 mm) from the end, and stop stitching ¼ inch (6 mm) from the other end.

2 Once again, place the pouch faceup. Position the zipper/side piece facedown (right sides together) along the top edge and side edges of the pouch back, easing and pinning the fabric to fit smoothly. Sew the patchwork zipper/side section to the back of the pouch. Start and stop stitching ¼ inch (6 mm) from the end of the patchwork section. Back tack at the beginning and at the end to secure the stitching.

NOTE: *The patchwork section will extend ¼ inch (6 mm) onto the bottom pouch section.*

3 Place the partially assembled pouch faceup. Position the front panel facedown on top of it (right sides together), and align the bottom edge of the front panel with the bottom panel of the pouch. Sew the bottom strip to the pouch front. Start stitching ¼ inch (6 mm) from the end, and stop stitching ¼ inch (6 mm) from the end.

4 Pin the front panel to the zipper/sides, easing the fabric to fit smoothly. Sew the pouch front to the side patchwork and zipper section. Start and stop stitching ¼ inch (6 mm) from the end of the patchwork section. Back tack at the start and at the end to secure the stitches.

5 With right sides facing each other, sew the bottom to the side of the pouch. Repeat for the opposite side.

6 Turn the pouch right side out and carefully press the seams to create creases.

ZIPPER PULL TAB

1 From the green fabric, cut a strip that measures 1 × 7 inches (2.5 × 17.8 cm).

2 Fold the strip in half along the 7-inch (17.8 cm) length and press.

3 Open the fold, fold each outer edge in toward the center crease, and press again.

4 Refold along the original center crease so that the raw edges are now tucked inside the fold. Sew close to the open edge, locking the raw edges inside the strip.

5 Loop the strip into the little hole in the zipper tab and tie into a knot.

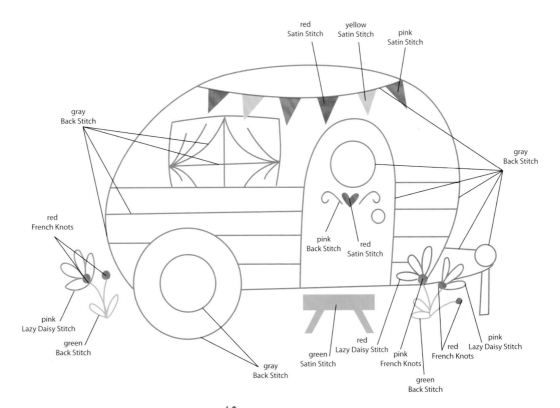

Tree Hill Canvas Frame Art

PROJECT DESIGNER
- - - - - - - - - - - - - - - -
AIMEE RAY

Stretching your stitching on a canvas frame is a great way to create artwork for display on your walls.

What You Need

3-5 different aqua blue patterned fabrics

3-5 different light green patterned fabrics

Motifs: tree, clouds, and hill (page 47)

1 piece of patterned white fabric, 6 × 6 inches (15.2 × 15.2 cm)

1 piece of plain white fabric, 6 × 6 inches (15.2 × 15.2 cm)
(This is a great way to use up scraps.)

Motifs: Embroidery pattern (page 47)

4 wooden canvas stretcher bars, 10 inches (25.4 cm) long

Staple gun and ¼-inch (6 mm) staples

Embroidery floss: 1 skein each of brown, green, and white

Stitches

Appliqué Stitch, Straight Stitch, Split Stitch, Satin Stitch, Long and Short Stitch

Instructions

1   Cut the aqua blue fabrics into squarish shapes approximately 3 × 4 inches (7.6 × 10.2 cm), and piece them together at random to create a square at least 12 × 12 inches (30.5 × 30.5 cm).

2   Piece the light green shapes together in the same way to create a hill shape according to the design (see design on page 47 and photo at left). Fold over ¼ inch (6 mm) of the top edge into a curve and press. Stitch the light green piece onto the aqua blue piece at the bottom using the Appliqué Stitch.

45

3   Sew a few more light green pieces together. Cut the oval shape for the tree from this piece. Stitch in place on the aqua blue background.

4   Trace and cut the cloud shapes from the patterned and plain white fabrics leaving ¼-inch (6 mm) seam allowance, and press the edges under. Stitch these in place on the aqua blue background.

5   Enlarge the embroidery pattern on page 47 by 115%. Then trace the pattern onto the fabric. Embroider the birds using 3 of the 6 threads of brown floss. Embroider the flowers and outlines of the tree and hill using all 6 threads of green floss.

6   Fit the frame bars together, and center the patchwork square over the frame. Fold the fabric edges over the frame, and staple them to the back side with one staple in the top and bottom and on either side. Then continue pulling the fabric tightly and stapling it down along each side of the frame.

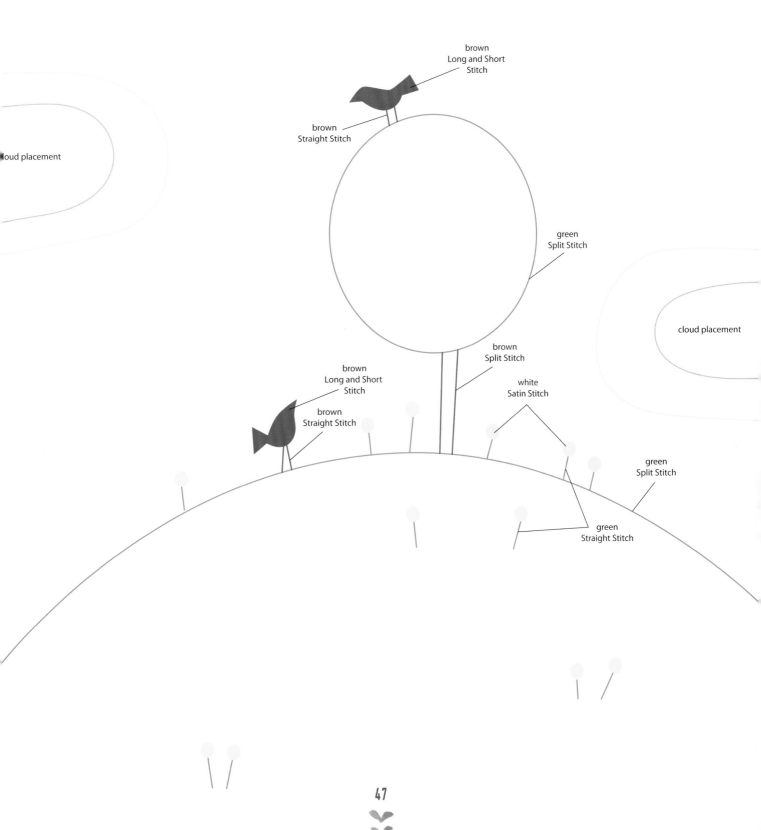

cloud placement

brown
Long and Short
Stitch

brown
Straight Stitch

green
Split Stitch

cloud placement

brown
Long and Short
Stitch

brown
Straight Stitch

brown
Split Stitch

white
Satin Stitch

green
Split Stitch

green
Straight Stitch

47

Cross Stitch Note Card

PROJECT DESIGNER

AIMEE RAY

Scrapbook paper and embroidery make this a unique note card to send to a special person.

What You Need

- 1 piece of cardstock or watercolor paper, 6 × 12 inches (15.2 × 30.5 cm)
- 3-5 different scrapbook papers in pinks and aquas
- White craft glue
- Motifs: Embroidery pattern (page 51)
- Carbon paper
- Embroidery floss: 1 skein each of pink, aqua, and turquoise
- Thimble

Stitches

Straight Stitch, Cross Stitch

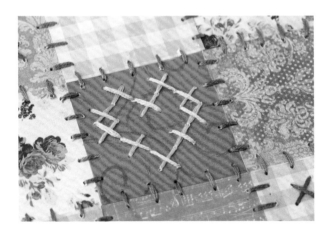

TIP

Stitching through paper can be hard on your fingers. Try wearing a rubber or leather thimble as you work, or use needle-nose pliers to pull/push the needle through the paper.

Instructions

1 Cut the cardstock, then score and fold it in the middle. Cut 9 squares from the scrapbook papers, 2 × 2 inches (5.1 × 5.1 cm) each, and arrange them on the front of the card. Glue them down, and let it dry.

2 Trace the embroidery pattern onto the card using carbon paper. If you're worried about getting carbon on the front of the card, you can trace it onto the back of the front panel instead.

3 Stitch the Cross Stitch design onto the corners of the card using 3 of the 6 threads of pink floss.

4 Stitch the Cross Stitch design in the center square using 3 of the 6 threads of aqua floss.

5 Using a Straight Stitch and 3 of the 6 threads of turqouise floss, stitch along the edges of the paper squares.

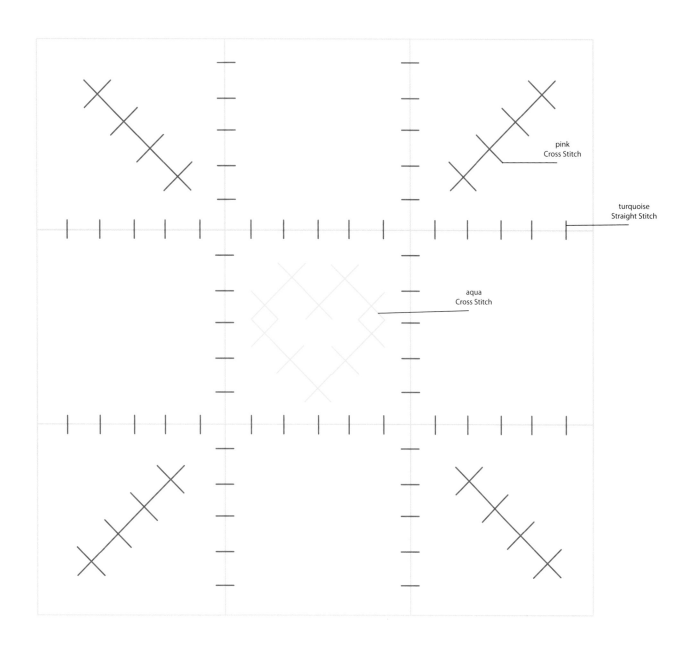

pink
Cross Stitch

turquoise
Straight Stitch

aqua
Cross Stitch

Cheery Cherry Kitchen Towel

PROJECT DESIGNER

AIMEE RAY

It's easy to brighten up any kitchen towel with a little patchwork appliqué and embroidery.

What You Need

3–5 different red and pink patterned fabrics cut to the following sizes:

    2 pieces, 3½ × 3½ inches (8.9 × 8.9 cm)

    2 pieces, 2½ × 3½ inches (6.4 ×8.9 cm)

    4 pieces, 2 × 3½ inches (5.1 × 8.9 cm)

Motifs: Embroidery patterns (page 55)

Carbon paper

Embroidery floss: 1 skein each of pink, light pink, and red

1 cream or white dish towel, 16 × 25 inches (40.6 × 63.5 cm) (Or sew your own by double-hemming the edge of a piece of fabric to this size.)

Stitches

Back Stitch, Satin Stitch

Instructions

1   Arrange the fabric pieces in a row as shown in the photo above, and sew them together. Seam allowances of ¼ inches are included in the dimensions. The finished strip should measure 16½ inches long by 3½ inches wide.

2   Using carbon paper, trace the embroidery patterns onto the fabrics. The designs should be the same size as shown on page 55. Then stitch the kitchen motifs according to the patterns using 3 of the 6 threads of floss.

3   Press the patchwork strip flat, folding under the top, bottom, and sides ¼ inch (6 mm). Pin it in place 2 inches (5.1 cm) from the bottom of the dish towel. Topstitch around the edge with red thread.

4   Transfer the cherries pattern to the bottom corner of the towel below the patchwork strip, and embroider it on.

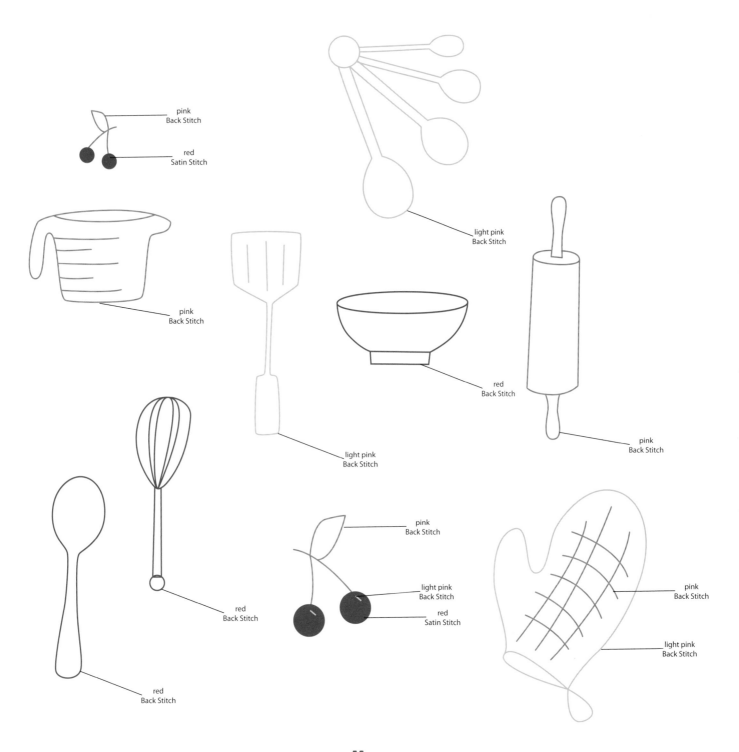

pink
Back Stitch

red
Satin Stitch

light pink
Back Stitch

pink
Back Stitch

pink
Back Stitch

red
Back Stitch

pink
Back Stitch

light pink
Back Stitch

red
Back Stitch

pink
Back Stitch

light pink
Back Stitch

red
Satin Stitch

pink
Back Stitch

light pink
Back Stitch

English Paper Piece Hexagon Hanging Hoop

PROJECT DESIGNER

CARINA ENVOLDSEN-HARRIS

The English paper piece hexagon is a very old quilting pattern that can be used to make any size project, from a small piece of wall art, as we are doing here, to a large quilt. The method uses small pieces that are extremely portable and can be taken anywhere to be worked on at any time, which helps to maintain its popularity today.

What You Need

Template: 7 piece paper hexagons, each 1³/4 inch (4.5 cm) across the shape, template (page 154)

1 sheet of plain copier paper

7 scraps of fabric in various light blue patterns, approx. 3 × 3 inches (7.6 × 7.6 cm)

Standard sewing needle

Basting thread

1 piece of fabric in a different light blue pattern for the background, minimum 13 inches (33 cm) in diameter

Carbon paper

Motifs: Embroidery pattern (page 59)

Embroidery floss: 1 skein each in dark blue, pink, and light blue

71 seed beads (or as many as you like)

3 buttons

1 hoop, 7 inches in diameter

1 piece of felt in matching color cut into a circle, 6¹/2 inches (16.5 cm) in diameter

Stitches

Hidden Stitch, Straight Stitch, Stem Stitch, Running Stitch, Cross Stitch, Basting Stitch, Whip Stitch

TIP

Your choice of fabric and floss colors will have a big effect on the final look of this project. You will see the best result if the background fabric and the hexagon fabric pieces are a light color. Use a dark color for the main embroidery floss, and use light to mid tones for the rest of the embroidery. For example, light blue fabrics with dark blue embroidery for the flower and light or mid-tone blue and pink for the accent stitching.

Instructions

TO MAKE THE ENGLISH PAPER PIECE HEXAGONS

1 First you will need to make the 7 English paper piece hexagons. Size each as indicated on page 154.

2 Using the hexagon template, copy it onto paper and cut out 7 hexagons. Be certain to make each hexagon exactly the same.

3 Place the hexagon template on the wrong side of the fabric. Pin 1 paper hexagon onto each of the 7 scraps of light blue patterned fabrics.

4 Cut around the paper templates, leaving ¼ inch (6 mm) extra fabric around all the edges. It is important to be precise with this step, as it will make the following steps easier to complete and deliver better results.

5 With the paper template securely pinned to the fabric, start along 1 edge and fold the fabric carefully up and over the paper, creating a straight folded edge.

6 While holding the first folded edge in place, move to an adjacent side and fold it up and over the paper as well.

7 Using a standard sewing needle and thread and a Basting Stitch, baste the fabric only at the corner to hold it in place. Take care not to sew the fabric to the paper.

8 Repeat this folding and basting along each edge of the hexagon until all sides have been folded over the paper edges and secured with the basting thread.

NOTE: *Making certain to create straight folds and crisp corners will ensure that your hexagons fit together perfectly.*

ASSEMBLE THE HEXAGON DESIGN

1   Press all the hexagons and then remove the paper templates.

2   Lay out the background circle of fabric faceup. Following the pattern on the hexagon placement template, pin the six hexagons in place onto the background fabric. Position and pin the single hexagon as well.

    NOTE: *You can also attach the hexagons using fusible webbing, but this is optional.*

3   Stitch the hexagons to the background fabric using a Hidden Stitch. (Alternatively, you could use Straight Stitches that will be visible if you want additional texture.)

EMBROIDER AND EMBELLISH THE DESIGN

1   Enlarge the flower motif 175%. Then transfer the pattern onto the face of the hexagons and the background fabric.

2   Embroider the flower using a Stem Stitch. Use longer stitches, so it's not too precise. The goal is to make the flower look a bit like a quick sketch on paper, so don't worry if the stitches aren't perfect. Imperfections add character.

3   When you have finished the embroidery, rinse out the transfer lines if necessary. Press the piece.

dark blue
Stem Stitch

4 Embroider rows of Running Stitch on the left side of the flower, embroidering across the background fabric and the hexagons. The rows don't have to perfectly straight—a bit of wonkiness adds more character as well as texture.

5 When you are happy with the area of Running Stitch, add Cross Stitches on top. Vary the size of the Cross Stitches.

6 Stitch seed beads loosely around the flower so they look as if they have been sprinkled on.

7 Sew three pretty buttons at the bottom of the flower.

FINISH WITH THE HOOP FRAME

1   Trim the fabric into the shape of a circle 11 inches (27.9 cm) in diameter.

2   Make a running Basting Stitch around the edge of the fabric ⅓ inch (8.5 mm) in. Place the fabric over the inner hoop.

   NOTE: *Use a long thread, at least 40 inches (101.6 cm), so there is plenty to use to draw the fabric closed and tie the ends together.*

3   Gently pull the two ends of the thread, working the fabric so that it gathers evenly toward the center of the hoop. When the fabric is snug to the frame, tie the ends tightly and cut off the excess thread.

4   Place the outer hoop over the fabric, smoothing the fabric at the edges. Align the screw at the top of the design and tighten.

5   Lay the framed design facedown. Place the felt circle over the gathered fabric on the back side and stitch in place using a Whip Stitch and matching color thread.

Patched Jeans

PROJECT DESIGNER

AIMEE RAY

When I finally wore a hole in the knee of my favorite old jeans, I was inspired to patch them using this fun technique I found online. You might even consider cutting a hole in your jeans just so you *have* to patch it.

What You Need

A pair of jeans with a hole in them

Liquid fray stopper

Piece of fabric 1 inch (2.5 cm) larger than the hole

Motifs: decorative embroidery designs (page 65)

Carbon paper

Embroidery floss: 1 skein each of light blue, medium blue, and dark blue

Stitches

Running Stitch, Back Stitch, Straight Stitch, Lazy Daisy Stitch, Satin Stitch, Split Stitch

Instructions

1 Trim away any extra long fray strings from around the hole in the jeans, and apply a generous amount of liquid fray stopper around the edge. Let it dry.

2 Slipping the cut fabric inside the jeans, place it over the hole and pin it in place. Make sure it covers the hole completely, with about 1 inch (2.5 cm) extra fabric overlapping the edge.

3 Make a couple of rows of Running Stitches around the edge of the hole to hold the fabric in place.

4 Using carbon paper, transfer the embroidery designs onto the jeans. The designs should be the same size as shown on page 65.

5 Following the stitch and color instructions on the motif, embroider the decorative stitching at the top and bottom of the hole. Use all 6 threads of floss.

NOTE: *This technique works best for holes not on the knee, where they will continue to get a lot of wear. If you want to patch a knee hole, you can cover the back of your fabric and embroidery with another piece of durable fabric using an iron-on adhesive.*

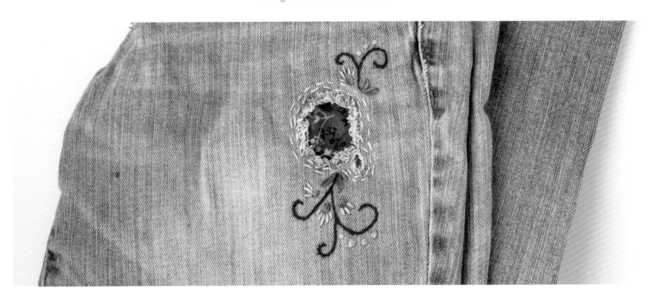

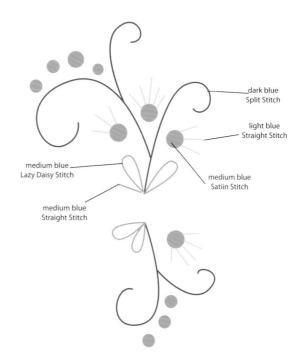

dark blue
Split Stitch

light blue
Straight Stitch

medium blue
Lazy Daisy Stitch

medium blue
Satiin Stitch

medium blue
Straight Stitch

I Sew Like a Boss Journal Cover

DESIGNER

ANNIE KIGHT

Use this fun journal cover to jot down sewing thoughts, ideas, sketches, and patterns. Let the creative juices flow!

What You Need

Templates: hexagon, rectangle, square, ruler (page 155)

2 sheets of plain copier paper

5 squares of scrap cotton prints in green, white, beige, light blue, and white, 2½ × 2½ inches (6.4 × 6.4 cm)

Short sewing pins

Standard sewing needle

Black thread for basting

Off-white thread

Iron

Embroidery scissors

Seam ripper

Tweezers

2 rectangular pieces of cotton fabric in taupe or beige for journal cover and lining, 17 × 9½ inches (43.2 × 24.1 cm)

Carbon paper

Motifs: "I Sew Like a Boss" lettering, tomato, stem, spool (page 70)

Embroidery hoop, 3 inches (7.6 cm) in diameter

Embroidery floss: 1 skein each of aqua, black, gray, white, red, green, yellow, and cream

(continued on the following page)

Stitches

Basting Stitch, Hidden Stitch, Whip Stitch, Back Stitch, Satin Stitch, French Knot, Straight Stitch

(continued from the previous page)

3 cute vintage-style buttons

1 piece of scrap print fabric in red for tomato pincushion, 2 × 2½ inches
(5.1 × 6.4 cm)

Liquid fray stopper

Fiber filler (approximately 3-square inches [7.6 cm] worth)

1 piece of printed fabric in yellow for ruler, 8 × 1½ inches (20.3 × 3.8 cm)

1 length of mini pompom trim in aqua, 51 inches (129.5 cm)

One hard-covered journal (110 pages), 5.75 × 8.75 × .75 inches
(14.6 × 22.2 × 1.9 cm)

Instructions

CONSTRUCTING THE SPINE

1   Size the hexagon template as indicated on page 155. Then copy the design
    5 times onto paper and cut out the 5 hexagons. Be certain to make each
    hexagon exactly the same.

2   Pin 1 paper hexagon onto each of the 5 scraps of cotton prints.

3   Cut around the paper templates, leaving ¼ inch (6 mm) extra fabric
    around all the edges. It is important to be precise with this step, as
    it will make the following steps easier to complete and deliver better
    results.

4   With the paper template securely pinned to the fabric, start along 1 edge
    and fold the fabric carefully up and over the paper, creating a straight
    folded edge.

5   While holding the first folded edge in place, move to an adjacent side,
    and fold it up and over the paper as well.

6   Using a standard sewing needle and thread and a Basting Stitch, baste
    only the fabric at the corner to hold it in place. Take care not to sew the
    fabric to the paper.

7   Repeat this folding and basting along each edge of the hexagon until all sides have been folded over the paper edges and secured with the basting thread.

   NOTE: *Making certain to create straight folds and crisp corners will ensure that your hexagons fit together perfectly.*

8   Arrange the 5 hexagons in a column as shown in the photo above. Hand-stitch the hexagons together using a Hidden Stitch and off-white thread.

9   Press the column with an iron set to the correct temperature for the fabrics used.

10   Remove all of the paper templates and basting thread using small embroidery scissors, a seam ripper, and tweezers as needed. Press the hexagon column again.

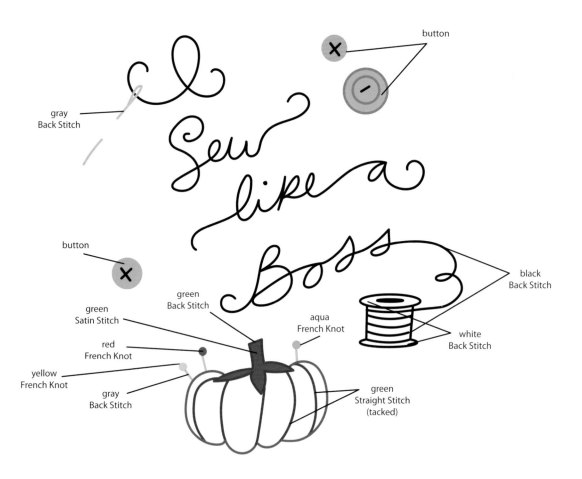

button

gray
Back Stitch

button

black
Back Stitch

green
Back Stitch

aqua
French Knot

white
Back Stitch

green
Satin Stitch

red
French Knot

yellow
French Knot

gray
Back Stitch

green
Straight Stitch
(tacked)

JOURNAL COVER AND LINING

1 Place the piece of journal cover fabric (17 × 9½ inches [43.2 × 24.1 cm]) facedown, and pin a ¼-inch (6 mm) seam allowance around all four sides.

2 Baste with black thread, and press with an iron.

3 Fold the journal cover in half (wrong sides facing and short sides aligned), and press a crease on the fold. This is where the spine of the journal will be.

4 Repeat step 3 using the second piece of 17 × 9½ inch (43.9 × 24.1 cm) fabric to create the journal lining. Set the journal lining aside for now.

5 Unfold the journal cover and place it faceup. Center the hexagon column along the crease, and pin it into place. The top hexagon and the bottom hexagon should line up perfectly with the basted hemlines.

6 Whip Stitch around each hexagon with aqua floss using two strands of floss.

STITCHING THE WORDS

1 Using the carbon paper, transfer the "I Sew Like a Boss" lettering onto the front of the journal cover. (Size as shown at left.) Use the photos as a guide for placement. Use a 3-inch embroidery hoop for all of the following decorative stitching.

2 Back Stitch the words in black using two strands of floss.

3 Back Stitch the thread spool top and bottom in white using two strands of floss.

4 Back Stitch the outer edges of the thread spool in black using two strands of floss.

5 Back Stitch the needle in gray using two strands of floss, but use one strand for the last stitch on the needle tip to make the needle appear "pointier."

6 Use two strands of black floss to sew the buttons into place.

NOTE: *Instead of sewing real buttons onto the cover, if you prefer, you could embroider the buttons using your choice of floss colors. Use the Satin Stitch for solid-colored buttons or the Back Stitch to simply create button-shaped outlines.*

TOMATO PINCUSHION

1 Using carbon paper, transfer the tomato template to the scrap of red printed fabric and cut it out. Apply liquid fray stopper around the edges and let it dry.

2 Pin the pincushion just to the bottom left of the embroidered thread spool (refer to photos for placement). Whip Stitch around the outer edge of the tomato with two strands of red floss, but leave a 1-inch (2.5 cm) opening.

3 Carefully insert little bits of fiber filler into the tomato using a pair of tweezers to desired firmness. Whip Stitch the opening closed using two strands of red floss.

4 Using carbon paper, transfer the tomato stem design into place, and Back Stitch the outer edges in green using two strands of floss. Fill in the stem with the same green floss using a Satin Stitch.

5 Use one strand of green floss to create the "sections" on the tomato pincushion. To make the sections appear curved, tack a tiny stitch along each of the 5 sections about midway down (refer to the photo at right).

6 Back Stitch the 3 sewing pins on the pincushion in gray using two strands of floss.

7 Stitch the pin tops in red, yellow, and aqua using French Knots and 2 strands of floss.

JOINING THE JOURNAL COVER AND LINING

1   Press the journal cover with an iron, and place it facedown on your working surface.

2   Baste the aqua mini pompom trim along the basted edges. The pompoms should be hanging just over the edges of the hemline. Make small folds at the corners with the pompom trim. Try to avoid bulkiness at the corners.

3   Now press the journal lining and place it faceup on top of the journal cover and pompom trim. Carefully pin the layers together. The pompom trim should be seen poking out along the perimeter on all four sides. Very slowly, machine stitch ⅛ inch (3.8 mm) in from the edges using the Straight Stitch setting. Try to keep the stitch line continuous by stopping and turning at each corner.

    NOTE: *Stitching slowly will ensure the pompom trim stays tucked in close to the edges.*

4   Remove the black basting thread and then Whip Stitch in between each pompom using two strands of floss in aqua.

CREATING THE JOURNAL POCKETS

1   Lay the journal cover facedown. Fold each of the short sides over 1½ inches (3.8 cm). This creates the pockets for the actual hard-covered journal to slip into. There is no need to press with an iron unless crisp edges are desired.

2   Position a ruler on the inside front flap of the cover (not shown). Size the ruler as indicated by the ruler template on page 155. Transfer the design to the 8 x 1½-inch (20.3 x 3.8 cm) yellow fabric and cut it out. Apply liquid fray stopper around the outer edges of the ruler and let it dry. Pin the ruler into place. Whip Stitch around the perimeter of the ruler using two strands of cream floss. Stitch the ruler "marker" lines using two strands of black floss.

3   Hand-stitch each of the four corners of the journal cover with two strands of floss in aqua.

4   Now it's time to insert the journal into the journal cover!

Pet Lover Wristband Keychains

PROJECT DESIGNER

AIMEE RAY

Show your love for kitty or pooch with these fun wristlet key chains.

What You Need

Carbon paper

Embroidery design motifs: *puppy love* lettering; *cat lady* lettering (page 77)

3-5 different scraps of orange or blue patterned fabrics (1 scrap must be at least 10½ inches [26.7 cm] long, and another scrap must be at least 5 inches [12.7 cm] square)

4-inch (10.2 cm) hoop

Embroidery floss: 1 skein each of dark orange, orange, dark blue, blue, and light blue

1¼-inch (32 mm) key ring for each wrist band

1 silver charm for each wristband

Instructions

1   Using the carbon paper, transfer the embroidery design to a piece of orange or blue fabric at least 5 inches (12.7 cm) square. The design should be the same size as shown on page 77. Using a 4-inch (10.2 cm) hoop, stitch the design according to the pattern stitches and colors using 3 of the 6 threads of floss.

2   Measure a 3½ × 1½ inch (8.9 × 3.8 cm) rectangle around the embroidery and cut it out.

Stitches

Back Stitch, Satin Stitch, Whip Stitch

It's a good idea to measure your wrist to see what circumference is easy to slip over your hand. You may need to add more squares for a larger band or use fewer squares for a smaller band. If you need to add or subtract squares for a proper fit, you will also need to adjust the 10½ × 1½-inch (26.7 × 3.8 cm) piece a corresponding amount so the two faces will match up perfectly.

3 Using different patterned fabrics, cut 1 piece, 10½ × 1½ inches (26.7 × 3.8 cm), for the inside of the band.

4 Using fabrics of various patterns, cut 7 1½ × 1½ inch (3.8 × 3.8 cm) pieces to complete the outside of the band. Using these pieces, the finished wristband will be a 9-inch (22.9 cm) circle.

5 Sew the embroidered 3½ × 1½-inch piece (8.9 x 3.8 cm) and the 7 pieces that measure 1½ × 1½ inches together in a row, placing 3 squares on one end and 4 squares on the other end of the embroidered piece.

6 Press the seams open and lay the assembled piece faceup.

7 Place the 10½ × 1½-inch (26.7 × 3.8 cm) piece facedown on top of the assembled piece (right sides together), and pin them together. Sew a ¼-inch (6 mm) seam along the long sides, stopping short of the ends by ½ inch (12 mm) and leaving both ends open.

8 Turn right side out and press.

9 Stitch ⅛ inch (3 mm) along the edges of the strip using the Whip Stitch or the Running Stitch. Stop stitching ½ inch (12 mm) before each end.

10 String a keychain onto the strip.

11 Turn the raw edges of one end into the inside of the strip, and then tuck the other end ¼ inch (6 mm) into the first end. Topstitch across the strip to secure them together.

12 Pull the keychain to the stitched end, and Topstitch across the strip 1 inch (2.5 cm) from the end.

13 Attach the charm to the keychain.

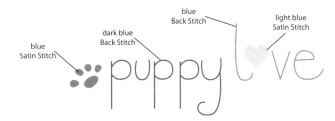

blue
Satin Stitch

dark blue
Back Stitch

blue
Back Stitch

light blue
Satin Stitch

puppy love

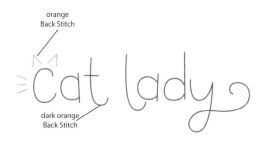

orange
Back Stitch

Cat lady

dark orange
Back Stitch

Lavender Hexagon Sachet

PROJECT DESIGNER

MOLLIE JOHANSON

Stitched with a bundle of lavender flowers and filled with the same, this hand-sewn sachet will keep your clothes smelling sweet. All it takes is a bit of embroidery and a few English paper piece hexagons!

What You Need

Carbon paper

Templates: 8 hexagon templates (page 154)

Embroidery design motif (page 81)

2 pieces of linen, 4 × 4 inches (10.2 × 10.2 cm)

3-inch (7.6 cm) embroidery hoop

Embroidery floss: 1 skein each in light violet and light green

Washable glue stick

6 different scraps of patterned fabrics in lavender, each at least 2½ inches square

Standard sewing needle and thread

Dried lavender, about ¼ ounce (7 g)

Instructions

EMBROIDER THE CENTRAL PANEL

1   Using the carbon paper, transfer the lavender embroidery design motif onto the center of 1 piece of linen. The design should be the same size as shown on page 81.

Stitches

Stem Stitch, Lazy Daisy Stitch, Back Stitch, Basting Stitch, Whip Stitch, Hidden Stitch

2   After fitting the linen into the embroidery hoop, embroider the design; use two strands of floss throughout. Use a Stem Stitch in light green for the stems, a Lazy Daisy Stitch in light violet for the petals, and a Back Stitch in light violet for the bow. Remove all the markings.

MAKE THE ENGLISH PAPER PIECE HEXAGONS

1   Size the hexagon template as indicated on page 154. Then copy the design onto paper 8 times and cut out the hexagons. Be certain to make each hexagon exactly the same.

2   Using a washable glue stick, glue 1 paper hexagon onto the back of each of the 2 pieces of linen. Be sure to center the embroidery design on the hexagon that is the front piece.

3   Glue 1 paper hexagon onto the backs of each of the 6 scraps of lavender patterned fabrics.

4   Cut outside the paper templates, leaving ⅜ inch (1 cm) extra fabric around all the edges as a seam allowance.

    NOTE: *It is important to be precise with this step, as it will make the following steps easier to complete and deliver better results.*

5   For each hexagon, with the paper template facing up, start along 1 edge and fold the fabric carefully up and over the paper, creating a straight folded edge.

6   While holding the first folded edge in place, move to an adjacent side and fold it up and over the paper as well.

7   Using a standard sewing needle and thread and a Basting Stitch, baste the fabric only at the corner to hold it in place. Take care not to sew the fabric to the paper.

8   Repeat this folding and basting along each edge of the hexagon until all sides have been folded over the paper edges and secured with the basting thread.

9   Repeat this process for each of the 8 hexagons.

    NOTE: *Making certain to create straight folds and crisp corners will ensure that your hexagons fit together perfectly.*

ASSEMBLE THE SACHET

1 Working on the back side, use a Whip Stitch to join one edge of each of the 6 lavender fabric hexagons to one edge of the embroidered hexagon.

2 Again working on the back side and using a Whip Stitch, join the adjacent sides of each lavender hexagon to the hexagon next to it. Stitch from the center panel out to the first point.

3 Continue working on the back side of the same two hexagons, joining the next set of sides by folding the hexagons inward until the edges meet.

4 Repeat with each set of adjacent lavender hexagons coming from the center panel. When 5 sides of each hexagon have been stitched, the assembled piece will look like a little bowl.

5 Fit the remaining plain linen hexagon into the center opening and Whip Stitch it in place, leaving two sides unstitched.

6 Remove the paper templates, and turn the sachet right side out.

7 Fill the sachet with dried lavender and stitch the opening closed using a Hidden Stitch.

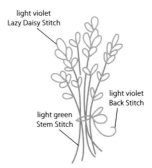

light violet
Lazy Daisy Stitch

light violet
Back Stitch

light green
Stem Stitch

Lunch Bag

PROJECT DESIGNER

TERESA MAIRAL BARREU

This lunch bag uses basic bargello quilting. Strips of fabric are sewn together, cut across into squares, and then positioned in a ladder similar to an Irish chain pattern. Dimensions of bag: 11 inches H × 9 inches W × 4½ inches D (27.9 × 22.9 × 11.4 cm) finished.

What You Need

Carbon paper

Embroidery design motifs: sandwich, salad bowl (page 87)

2 pieces gray linen, 11 × 10 inches (27.9 × 25.4 cm), for the salad bowl and for the sandwich

Embroidery floss: 1 skein each in ombré green, red, brown, cream, purple, tan, brown, and orange

3 pieces Irish Chain Patchwork (to make these pieces, see instructions on the next page)

3 pieces of fabric in different colors or patterns, each measuring 4½ × 17 inches (11.4 × 43.2 cm)

Medium-weight fusible interfacing

1 piece dark green fabric to use for the bottom of the bag, 5 × 9½ inches (12.7 × 24.1 cm)

1 piece dark green striped fabric to use as the lining of the bag, 27½ × 9½ inches (69.9 × 24.1 cm)

2 pieces dark green fabric to use as the sides of the bag, 10½ × 5 inches (26.7 × 12.7 cm)

2 pieces dark green striped fabric to use as the lining of the sides of the bag, 10½ × 5 inches (26.7 ×12.7 cm)

1 strip of white hook and loop tape, 4 inches (10.2 cm) × ¾ inch (2 cm)

Pins

About 66 inches (167.6 cm) of bias tape, 1½ inches (38.1 cm) wide

Seam ripper

Stitches

Stem Stitch, Back Stitch, French Knots, Long and Short Stitch, Whipped Back Stitch

Embroider Front and Back Panels

1   Enlarge the sandwich design motif to 200% of the size shown on page 87. Using the carbon paper, transfer the design onto 1 piece of gray linen, making certain to position the design on the fabric so that it will appear centered once the flap is overlapped at the top.

   NOTE: *The finished sandwich piece will be bigger than the salad bowl piece to accommodate the folded-over flap hiding some of the linen fabric at the top. Take this into consideration as you position the design template on the fabric by lowering the design an additional 2 inches (5.1 cm) from the top edge.*

2   Embroider the sandwich as follows: lettuce using a Stem Stitch in ombré green, tomato using a Stem Stitch in red, bread using a Stem Stitch in brown, mayo using a Back Stitch in cream, and bread seeds using French Knots in brown.

3   When the stitching is complete, trim the gray linen to measure 8 × 9½ inches (20.3 × 24.1 cm).

4   Enlarge the salad bowl design motif to 175% of the size shown on page 87. Using the carbon paper, transfer the design template onto the second piece of gray linen, taking care to center the design.

5   Embroider the salad bowl as follows: olives using a Long and Short Stitch in purple, bowl using a Whipped Back Stitch and French Knots in tan/ brown, carrot sticks using a Back Stitch in orange, tomato using a Stem Stitch in red, and fork using a Stem Stitch in tan/brown.

6   When the stitching is complete, trim the gray linen to measure 6 × 9½ inches (15.2 × 24.1 cm).

Irish Chain Patchwork Pieces Instructions

1   Cut 3 strips from each fabric measuring 1½ × 17 inches (3.8 × 43.2 cm).

2   Lay the strips out side by side lengthwise, alternating the fabrics in repeating order. Sew the strips together lengthwise, one after the other, taking care to keep the order for the three fabrics. You will end up with a rectangle measuring 9½ × 17 inches (24.1 × 43.2 cm).

3   Press the pieced strips with the seams open to reduce bulk.

4 Fold the piece in half lengthwise with the right sides facing together to make a rectangle measuring 4¾ × 17 inches (12 × 43.2 cm). Sew along the long side to create a tube.

5 Now cut across the tube, creating strips measuring 1½ inches (3.8 cm) wide. You will end up with 11 strips.

NOTE: For the following steps, it will really help if you keep the strips laid out in order as they were cut from the tube with the final seam used to sew the tube positioned away from you. Pick up only one piece at a time and replace it before working on the next.

6 Pick up the first strip, and, using a seam ripper, remove the seam at the top of the strip (the one that you just sewed to make the large piece into a tube). Open the strip and press it flat.

7 Looking at the second piece, locate the seam that lies one square closer to you. Remove this seam, which is one square away from the last seam you ripped out. Open the strip and press it flat. Notice that if you overlap the pieces, you can see a ladder starting to form.

8 Repeat this process for each of the remaining strips. Move down one square each time to locate the proper seam to remove.

NOTE: For the bag you will need 3 separate pieces of patchwork. The bottom front and bottom back pieces are the same; they use 3 strips stitched together into a rectangle. The flap piece uses 4 strips pieced together into a larger rectangle.

9 Take the first 2 strips and align them right sides together (face to face). Sew them together lengthwise.

10 Pick up the third strip and align it right sides together with the second strip. Sew together lengthwise.

11 Open this 3-strip rectangle and press the seams open.

12 Repeat steps 8–10 to create a second 3-strip rectangle.

13 Returning to the remaining strips, pick up the next 2 strips in order, place them right sides together (face to face), and sew together lengthwise.

14 Pick up the next strip, align it right sides together over the preceding strip, and sew together lengthwise.

15 Pick up the last strip, align it right sides together over the preceding strip, and sew together lengthwise.

16 Open this 4-strip rectangle and press the seams open.

ASSEMBLING THE BAG

1   First, lay out the following pieces faceup and end to end in the order listed.

   a. Sandwich embroidery

   b. 1 piece of 3-row patchwork rectangle

   c. Dark green fabric cut to bottom of bag

   d. 1 piece of 3-row patchwork rectangle

   e. Salad bowl embroidery with its top oriented in the opposite direction from the sandwich

   f. 4-row patchwork rectangle that becomes the lunch bag flap

   NOTE: *Be sure that the embroidery pieces are properly oriented in opposite directions. Once the faces are folded upright to make the front and back of the bag, you want both designs to be facing right side up.*

2   Starting with the first 2 pieces, position them right sides together, and sew along the 9½-inch (24.1 cm) long side using a ¼-inch (6 mm) seam allowance.

3   Repeat this step for each of the remaining pieces until you have assembled a long rectangle for the outside of the bag.

4   Press the seams open.

5   Following the manufacturer's instructions, cut and apply medium-weight fusible interfacing to the back side of the rectangle that you just assembled and pressed.

6   Take the dark green striped fabric lining piece (27½ × 9½ inches [69.9 × 24.1 cm]), and, following the manufacturer's instructions, apply medium-weight fusible interfacing to the back side of the fabric.

7   Take the 2 pieces of dark green fabric for the sides of the bag and apply the fusible interfacing to the back of each piece.

NOTE: *Do not apply the fusible interfacing to the lining pieces of the sides of the bag. Use only one piece of interfacing for each side so that the sides are more malleable than the body.*

8 Now add the hook and loop tape.

9 Turn the rectangle over with the sandwich facing up, and place one side of the hook and loop tape on the face of the gray linen. Center it. Align it parallel to and set back from the edge about ¾ inch (1.9 cm).

10 Cut the lining piece (27½ × 9½ inches) in the dark green striped fabric and a piece of medium-weight fusible interfacing the same size, and iron following the manufacturer's instructions.

11 Then position the opposite piece of the hook and loop tape centered on the lining side of the front flap at ¾ inch (19 mm) from the edge.

12 Check to make certain that the 2 sides of tape match up well. Sew it in place.

13 Place the lining piece and assembled piece wrong sides facing together and sew together, leaving ¼ inch seam (6 mm) allowance.

14 Stitch bias tape to the narrow side of the large rectangle and to one of the narrow sides of each side rectangle.

15 Align the top of one side piece with the narrow side of the rectangle on the salad bowl side, lining side facing together. Sew in place.

16 Repeat on the other side.

17 To stitch the sides, align each side with the lining sides facing and pin the edges together. Sew around the bag with allowance for a seam of ¼ inch (6 mm).

18 Apply bias tape to cover all the raw edges.

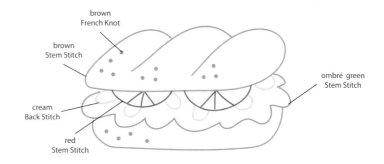

brown
French Knot

brown
Stem Stitch

ombré green
Stem Stitch

cream
Back Stitch

red
Stem Stitch

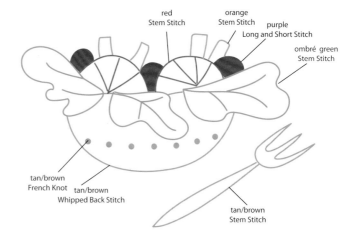

red
Stem Stitch

orange
Stem Stitch

purple
Long and Short Stitch

ombré green
Stem Stitch

tan/brown
French Knot

tan/brown
Whipped Back Stitch

tan/brown
Stem Stitch

Mandala Color Wheels Table Mat

PROJECT DESIGNER

MOLLIE JOHANSON

It's a color explosion! This table mat has a rainbow of stitches and a rainbow of patchwork. With colorful rings sewn by hand using English paper piecing, you can enjoy a bit of peace and stillness as you piece it all together.

Materials

White fabric for embroidery, 8 × 8 inches (20.3 × 20.3 cm)

Embroidery design (page 157)

Water-soluble marker or carbon paper

7-inch (17.8 cm) embroidery hoop

Embroidery floss: 1 skein each of red, orange, yellow, light green, medium blue-green, and purple (or colors to match fabric)

Templates: small, medium, and large arcs, 12 each; 1 circle (pages 156-157)

Cardstock

Iron

Washable glue stick

Needle and thread

6 quilting cottons in a rainbow of hues, 9 × 21 inches (22.9 × 53.3 cm) each

Masking tape

Quilting cotton for backing, 2/3 yard (.6 meter)

Cotton batting, 21 × 21 inches (53.3 × 53.3 cm)

Pins

White perle cotton, no. 8

Stitches

Stem Stitch, Back Stitch, Lazy Daisy Stitch, French Knot, Satin Stitch, Running Stitch, Whip Stitch, Ladder Stitch

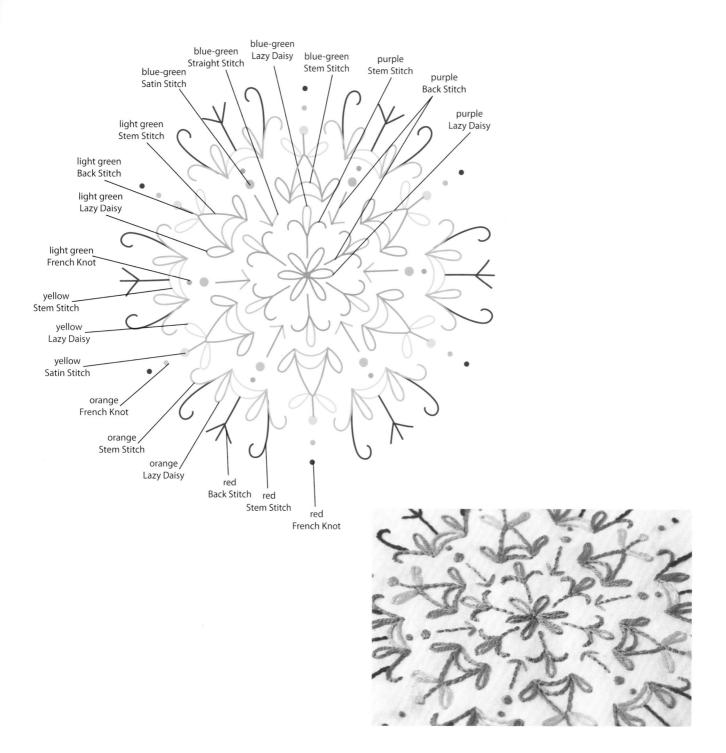

blue-green
Straight Stitch

blue-green
Lazy Daisy

blue-green
Satin Stitch

blue-green
Stem Stitch

purple
Stem Stitch

purple
Back Stitch

light green
Stem Stitch

purple
Lazy Daisy

light green
Back Stitch

light green
Lazy Daisy

light green
French Knot

yellow
Stem Stitch

yellow
Lazy Daisy

yellow
Satin Stitch

orange
French Knot

orange
Stem Stitch

orange
Lazy Daisy

red
Back Stitch

red
Stem Stitch

red
French Knot

90

Instructions

1 Size the mandala design as indicated on page 157. Using the light box method and water-soluble marker or carbon paper, trace the design onto the white fabric.

2 Fit the fabric into the hoop, and embroider the design. Use three strands of floss throughout. Stitch the curved lines with Stem Stitch, the straight lines with Back Stitch, the petals with Lazy Daisy Stitch, the small dots with French Knots, and the large dots with Satin Stitch.

3 Remove all the markings.

4 Size the template shapes as indicated on page 156 and 157. Trace or print the shapes onto cardstock, then cut them out. You will need 1 center circle and 12 of each of the 3 arc sizes. It is very important that the pieces be accurate.

5 Position the circle template on the back of the embroidery, centering it. Use a washable glue stick to hold it in place. Cut around the template, leaving a 1/2-inch (13 mm) seam allowance. Use a needle and thread to make large Running Stitches around the seam allowance, then pull the thread to gather and tighten the fabric around the template. If the embroidery isn't centered, loosen the template from the fabric and shift it slightly to center it. Press the edges.

6 Use a washable glue stick to hold the arc templates to the back of the six quilting cotton fabrics. Place the pieces so the curve of the template is on the fabric bias. You will need two of each size arc from each of the six colors. Cut around the templates, leaving a 3/8-inch (10 mm) seam allowance.

7 Baste the center circle and the arcs. Wrap the seam allowance to the back of the templates, and use needle and thread to stitch through the fabric and templates, holding it in place. Take a stitch every 3/4 inch (1.9 cm) or so. The seam allowance is already wrapped on the circle (from step 5), but you still need to baste through the fabric and template.

8 Join the arcs together in rainbow order, making sections of 6 arcs to form halves of the different-size rings. Hold 2 pieces right sides together, aligning the edges, and sew the seam with Whip Stitch.

TIPS

Take care to remove the masking tape when you take a stitching break so it doesn't leave any residue on the fabric.

Using a very thin needle will help make your stitches less visible.

9   Join the smallest ring halves to the center circle. Use masking tape on the right side of the fabric to hold the pieces butted up next to each other. Use Whip Stitch on the back of the work to sew the pieces together. It helps to start at the center of the ring half and work toward the end, then start again from the center and work out to the other end. Repeat this with the other ring half, then join the straight ends. Continue adding the remaining ring halves in the same way.

10 When the entire top is joined together, iron the seam allowances on the back and around the edge, then remove the basting stitches and templates. Gently iron the seam allowance open along the edge, but do not press out the creases.

11 Cut the backing fabric and batting to match the pieced front. Layer the pieces together with the batting on the bottom, the backing (right side up), and then the top (wrong side up). Pin around the edge. Sew around the circle, stitching in the crease left from the edge of the templates, leaving a 4-inch (10.2 cm) opening for turning. Be sure to Back Stitch at the start and stop.

12 Turn the table mat right side out, and sew the opening closed with Ladder Stitch.

13 Hand-quilt around the center circle and each ring with white perle cotton using a Running Stitch. Pop the knots through the back to hide them.

Mushroom Pincushion & Mini Mushroom Pin Toppers

PROJECT DESIGNER

ANNIE KIGHT

What You Need for the Mushroom Pincushion

Carbon paper

Templates: 19 hexagon templates, ½ inch (1.3 cm) (page 158)

Embroidery design: door, window (page 158)

1 sheet plain copier paper

19 pieces cotton fabric, each at least 1½ inches (3.8 cm) square in light pink, light blue, tan, beige, taupe, and off-white

Black thread for basting

Off-white thread for stitching finished hexagons together

Needles

Small embroidery scissors

Seam ripper

Tweezers

Iron

2 circles of taupe cotton or flax fabric, 5 inches (12.7 cm) in diameter, for mushroom top and mushroom underbelly

Liquid fray stopper

Embroidery floss: 1 skein each of very light beige, light salmon, dark salmon, and bright chartreuse

Small sewing pins

Fiber filler

Long dollmaker's needle

(continued on the following page)

Stitches

Appliqué Stitch, Back Stitch, Lazy Daisy Stitch, French Knot, Basting Stitch

(continued from the previous page)

One piece taupe cotton or flax fabric matching the mushroom top and mushroom underbelly, 4 × 4 inches (10.2 × 10.2 cm) square, for mushroom stem

One piece thin interface, 4 × 4 inches (10.2 × 10.2 cm) square

One piece beige or taupe cotton fabric matching the center hexagon of the mushroom top, 2 × 2 inches (5.1 × 5.1 cm) square, for door and window

One sturdy bamboo skewer/stick

Kitchen shears

Craft glue

One wood base, 5 inches (12.7 cm) square

Flat-edge craft paint brush

Beige craft paint

Satin finish varnish

Drill and drill bit sized to the diameter of the skewer

One piece of green felt, 4½ × 4½ inches (11.4 × 11.4 cm) square

Scalloped fabric scissors (for cutting the edges of the green felt)

White craft glue

Small assorted pebbles and tumbled glass

Glitter or white sand

Cotton swabs

Two colors of green wool roving for moss mounds

Felting needle

1 small chunk upholstery foam in various sizes

Felting alternative: 1 piece moss green felt, 2½ × 5 inches (6.4 × 12.7 cm)

Toothpick

6 small posies or velvet flowers

Instructions for the Mushroom Pincushion

CONSTRUCTING THE MUSHROOM TOP

1   Size the hexagon template as indicated on page 158. Copy it onto paper 19 times and cut out the 19 hexagons. Be certain to make each hexagon exactly the same.

2   Pin 1 paper hexagon onto each of the 19 pieces of cotton fabric.

3   Cut around the paper templates, leaving ¼ inch (6 mm) extra fabric around all the edges. It is important to be precise with this step, as it will make the following steps easier to complete and deliver better results.

4   With the paper template securely pinned to the fabric, start along 1 edge and fold the fabric carefully up and over the paper, creating a straight folded edge.

5   While holding the first folded edge in place, move to an adjacent side and fold it up and over the paper as well.

6   Using a standard sewing needle with black thread and a Basting Stitch, baste the fabric only at the corner to hold it in place. Take care not to sew the fabric to the paper.

7   Repeat this folding and basting along each edge of the hexagons until all sides have been folded over the paper edges and secured with the basting thread.

    NOTE: *Creating straight folds and crisp corners will ensure that your hexagons fit together perfectly.*

8   Arrange the hexagons in the pattern shown in the illustration on the facing page. Use a plain beige or taupe hexagon in the center. Hand-stitch all of the hexagons together using off-white or beige thread. Press with an iron to help keep the corners crisp. Remove all of the paper templates and black basting thread with tweezers, a seam ripper, and small embroidery scissors if needed. Press again.

9   Apply liquid fray stopper to the outer edges of the mushroom top and mushroom underbelly circles. Let them dry.

10   Pin the hexagon cluster faceup onto the mushroom top circle (also faceup). Appliqué Stitch around the outer edges of the hexagons first, then Appliqué Stitch around each hexagon.

11 Embroider a small flower in the plain center hexagon and another small flower around the outer edge. Back Stitch the flower stem and Lazy Daisy Stitch the leaves using chartreuse. Lazy Daisy Stitch the flower petals using light salmon. Stitching only the flower along the outside edge of the assembled hexagons, create French Knots in the center of the flower using dark salmon. For now, do not stitch the center of the flower that is located on the central hexagon—leave it unfinished.

12 Pin the mushroom top circle right side down on top of the mushroom underbelly circle right side up (faces together). Machine-stitch around the outer edges, allowing a ¼-inch (6 mm) seam allowance. Leave a 2-inch (5.1 cm) opening for stuffing, and trim around the edges. Carefully turn right side out, and fill the mushroom top with fiber filler to desired firmness. Turn in a ¼-inch (6 mm) seam allowance at the opening, and pin if necessary. Hand-stitch the opening closed using off-white or beige thread, and reshape, if needed, to evenly distribute the fiber filler.

13 Flip the mushroom top upside down, and find the center of the underbelly. Thread a long dollmaker's needle with off-white or beige thread, and find the center on the other side right where the flower middle is. Sew a few stitches up and down through the center to create a tufted mushroom top. Tie off the thread on the underbelly side. Now it's time to French Knot the center of the flower in the middle of the top of the mushroom using dark salmon floss.

CONSTRUCTING THE MUSHROOM STEM

1 Lay the 4 × 4-inch (10.2 × 10.2 cm) square of taupe cotton or flax fabric facedown, lay the 4 × 4-inch (10.2 × 10.2 cm) square of interfacing on top, and pin together. Turn the bottom edge up ¼ inch (6 mm), pin, and machine-stitch the hem. Repeat this step for the top hem on the opposite edge of the fabrics.

2 Size the door and window designs as indicated on page 158. Then transfer the designs onto a 2 × 2-inch (5.1 × 5.1 cm) square of plain beige or taupe cotton. Apply liquid fray stopper around the edges and let them dry. Center the door along the bottom of the mushroom stem just above the hemline and baste in place with a couple of stitches.

3 Position the window to the right of the door as shown in the photo on the facing page, and baste in place.

4   Embroider the mushroom stem using 2 threads of floss. Using very light beige, Appliqué Stitch around the edge of the door and Back Stitch the door panels. Using very light beige, Back Stitch around the edge of the window and window panes. Lazy Daisy Stitch the flower petals with light salmon. French Knot the centers of the flowers at the base of the window and at the tops of the stems along with the doorknob using dark salmon. Lazy Daisy Stitch all of the grass leaves, and Back Stitch the flower stems along the bottom edge using bright chartreuse. Keep all of your stitches just above the hemline. Lazy Daisy Stitch the flower petals below the window and on the stems using light salmon.

5   Once the embroidery is complete on the mushroom stem, fold in half and pin together along the unfinished sides with the wrong side facing out. Machine-stitch a ¼-inch (6 mm) seam allowance to close. Turn right side out. The mushroom stem should resemble a tube.

6   Fill the tube firmly with fiber filler, and carefully insert a skewer through the center of the tube, pointy side down. Add more fiber filler around the skewer. Trim off both the sharp end and the top of the skewer with a heavy-duty pair of kitchen shears. Leave ¼ inch (6 mm) of the skewer sticking out from each end of the filled tube.

7   Stitch a few times back and forth across the top of the mushroom stem to create a web-like design. Make sure the top of the skewer stays above the top of the hemline. Repeat this step for the bottom of the stem.

8   Turn the mushroom top over so the underbelly is facing up. Apply some craft glue in the tufted center area. Be careful not to extend the glue beyond the diameter of the mushroom stem. Apply a small amount of craft glue to the top of the mushroom stem. Join the top of the stem to the underbelly of the mushroom. The skewer should be nestled into the very center of the tufted underbelly of the mushroom. Keep the mushroom turned upside down to dry overnight. After the glue has dried, hand-sew a few stitches around the top of the stem and the underbelly of the mushroom for extra support.

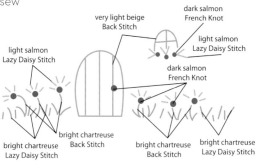

very light beige
Back Stitch

dark salmon
French Knot

light salmon
Lazy Daisy Stitch

light salmon
Lazy Daisy Stitch

dark salmon
French Knot

bright chartreuse
Back Stitch

bright chartreuse
Lazy Daisy Stitch

bright chartreuse
Back Stitch

bright chartreuse
Lazy Daisy Stitch

99

ATTACHING THE MUSHROOM TO THE WOOD BASE

1   Paint the wood base a neutral beige or taupe color with craft paint to complement the colors of the mushroom. Let it dry, and then apply a satin varnish to the top and sides of the wood base.

2   Paint the underside of the base, but only around the outer edges about 1 inch (2.5 cm) wide. Let it dry. Varnish the bottom to cover where the beige paint is. Let it dry again.

3   Drill a hole the same size diameter of the skewer in the upper-left corner of the top of the wood base. Drill only the depth, or a little more, that the skewer protrudes from the bottom of the mushroom stem—about ¼ inch (6 mm) deep. Do not to drill all the way through to the bottom.

4   Using the scalloped fabric scissors, trim a decorative edge around the 4½ × 4½-inch (11.4 × 11.4 cm) square piece of green felt.

5   Turn the wood base upside down. Apply craft glue sparingly to the outer edges of the trimmed piece of green felt and attach to the bottom of the wood base. Let it dry. Turn the base right side up and fill the hole with a small drop of craft glue. Apply some glue to the bottom of the mushroom stem. Try to avoid extending the glue beyond the edges of the stem so it doesn't seep out. Turn the mushroom right side up and insert the skewer into the hole while pushing down gently. Let it dry.

CREATING THE COBBLESTONE PATHWAY

1   Drizzle a pathway with hot glue, and arrange small pebbles and tumbled glass to resemble cobblestone as seen in the photo at the left. Make sure the glue is somewhat thick so it comes up between the stones. Work as quickly as possible. Sprinkle the pathway with glitter or sand while the glue is still wet. Let it sit for a few minutes, and then gently knock off the excess. Let this dry for a few hours or overnight.

2   Water down some craft paint in a beige or neutral tone, and carefully wash over the pathway to color the "grout" in between the stones and glass. Pay special attention to the base of the mushroom stem where the front door is, and make sure not to get the watered-down paint on the fabric. Let this dry for a few hours. As the paint dries, it will leave a haze over the pebbles and glass. Take cotton swabs dipped in water and polish the stones back to a pretty sheen. Once this is dry, paint over the pathway with satin varnish.

CREATING THE MOSS MOUNDS

1 Making moss mounds is fun and easy! Start with small balls of rolled-up wool roving, and poke and stab the balls with a felting needle onto a piece of upholstery foam until the desired shape and size is achieved. Create five different mounds using two colors of green to add a little depth and dimension. Each mound should be no less than ½ inch (1.3 cm) high. It will work best if you keep one side of each mound flat.

2 Apply craft glue to the flat side of each mound, and place on top of the wood base as seen in the photo at the right.

   NOTE: *As an alternative to felted moss mounds, you can cut moss green felt into 5 small shapes. Apply glue very sparingly around the outer edges of the felt moss shapes, leaving a small opening. Let them dry. Insert small amounts of fiber filler into the opening with tweezers, moving it into place with a toothpick or skewer until desired firmness is achieved. Glue the opening closed.*

3 To finish the mushroom pincushion, randomly glue 6 small posies or velvet flowers around the bases of the moss mounds.

What You Need for the Pin Toppers

NOTE: *To make the pin toppers, you will need a way to bake clay materials. A toaster oven works well if you prefer to not heat plastics in the oven you use for cooking food. A good pair of oven mitts will make handling hot materials easier.*

Mini loaf pan

Coarse rock salt (enough to fill loaf pan)

6 two-inch corsage pins with pearls on top

Very sharp, small knife

6 short sewing pins with tiny silver heads

Wire cutter

White polymer clay for mushroom stems and mushroom tops

Flat, clean surface such as a piece of glass or smooth tabletop

Tweezers

Small chunk of Styrofoam™ to hold pins in place

Toothpicks

(continued on the following page)

(continued from the previous page)

Liquid polymer clay

Pliers

Clear satin varnish

Small paint brush

Craft paint in pale pink, pale yellow, pale blue, pale aqua, tan, brown, sage green, moss green, mint green, lemon lime, peach, and mauve

Instructions for the Pin Topper

1   Preheat the oven to 265° Fahrenheit (129.4° Celsius), and fill the mini loaf pan with coarse rock salt all the way to the brim.

2   Crush the plastic pearls on the tops of the corsage pins until they become loose from the pins. Remove the pearls and run a sharp knife over the pin tops to clean off the residual plastic coating.

3   Snip off the tiny silver heads from the short sewing pins with a wire cutter.

SCULPTING THE STEMS

1   Roll 12 small white balls of clay about 1/16 inch (2 mm) in diameter on a clean, smooth surface. Once the balls are rolled, let them sit for a few minutes. Use your index fingertip to roll the balls into a shape that resembles an elongated cone to serve as the mushroom stems. Insert the tops of the pins up into the bottom of the stems. After each pin is inserted into the clay stem bottom, use a pair of tweezers to transfer the pins onto a chunk of Styrofoam. Try not to touch the clay.

SCULPTING MUSHROOM CAPS

1   Roll 12 small balls of white clay about 3/32 inch (3 mm) in diameter on a smooth surface. Once the balls are rolled, let them sit for a few minutes. Gently press the balls to resemble a sphere cut in half. Turn the caps over, and make small, shallow cuts with a sharp paring knife to resemble the underbelly of a mushroom.

2   Poke a tiny hole with a toothpick in the center of each underbelly. Dab a very small dot of liquid polymer clay into the holes of each mushroom cap. Gently attach each mushroom cap to each mushroom stem.

3   Transfer each completed mushroom with a pair of tweezers into the mini loaf pan filled with coarse rock salt. Avoid touching the clay with fingers or hands.

4   Bake mushrooms for 20 to 30 minutes. Turn off the oven and let the mushrooms cool in the oven for about an hour or until they are able to be handled. Remove them from the oven, and let them cool to room temperature.

5   Apply a thin coat of clear satin varnish to the mushrooms—don't forget the bottom of the stem and the underbelly of the cap! Insert them into the Styrofoam block with a pair of tweezers, and let them dry for about an hour.

6   Using a variety of craft paints, paint each mushroom cap a different color, but try not to paint the underbelly. Leave the stems white, and let them dry again.

7   Dip the end of a toothpick into white craft paint to create tiny polka dots all over the mushroom caps, and let them dry.

8   Finish the mushrooms with one more coat of thin clear varnish, and let them dry.

9   Arrange the mushroom pin toppers in the moss mounds or on the top of the tufted mushroom pincushion!

Scrappy Owl

PROJECT DESIGNER

AIMEE RAY

This cute owl plush is easy to sew without following a lot of rules. You can use what you have to create a whole parliament of owls in different sizes and colors.

What You Need

Templates: owl body, eye, and nose (page 159)

Embroidery design motif: flower (page 107)

A bunch of felt scraps in different colors

Embroidery floss: 1 skein each of ecru, brown, and pink

Pinking shears

2 buttons

Carbon paper

Embroidery design motif: flower

White chalk

Stuffing

Stitches

Whip Stitch, Running Stitch, Back Stitch, French Knot, Lazy Daisy Stitch, Satin Stitch

Instructions

1   Size the owl body template as indicated on page 159, or draw your own. Make a tall skinny owl or a short fat one. Don't worry about making it too perfect; imperfect shapes give your owl more character. Cut out the shape.

2   Assemble your scraps by roughly organizing them into a shape big enough to cover your template. You'll need to do this twice, for a front and a back piece.

3   Start stitching your scraps together using 3 strands of floss. Overlap the edges ¼ to ½ inch (6 to 13 mm), and stitch them together using the Whip Stitch. Don't worry about being too neat; messy is unique.

4   When you've got two pieces of patchwork felt big enough to cover your template with about ½ inch (1.3 cm) around the edges, determine which you'll use as the front, and add the face. Use pinking shears to cut the two eye circles, and stitch them on with the Running Stitch in 3 strands of ecru floss. Then sew on the buttons over the eye circles. Stitch the beak on at the top between the eyes using 3 strands of brown floss.

5   The flower embroidery pattern motif should be the same size as shown on page 107. Using the carbon paper, transfer it onto the felt.

6   Embroider the flower motif according to the pattern using 3 of the 6 threads of floss.

7   Now pin the front and back together, right sides facing, and trace on the template with white chalk. Sew around the edges using a sewing machine, and leave the bottom open.

8   Turn it right side out, stuff, and sew up the bottom using a Whip Stitch and colored floss.

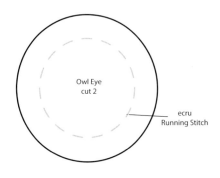

Owl Eye
cut 2

ecru
Running Stitch

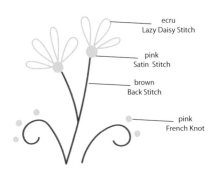

ecru
Lazy Daisy Stitch

pink
Satin Stitch

brown
Back Stitch

pink
French Knot

Satin Panda Pillow

PROJECT DESIGNER
AIMEE RAY

Satin fabrics are so luxurious, perfect for an unusual take on patchwork on this pretty and comfortable pillow.

What You Need

- 2 pieces of red patterned satin, 3½ × 5 inches (8.9 × 12.7 cm)
- 2 pieces of pink patterned satin, 3½ × 5 inches (8.9 × 12.7 cm)
- 2 pieces of purple patterned satin, 3¾ × 5 inches (9.5 × 12.7 cm)
- 1 piece of lavender satin, 5½ × 11 inches (14.0 × 27.9 cm)
- Embroidery design motif: panda, flower (page 111)
- Tissue paper
- 1 piece of lavender satin, 11 × 15½ inches (27.9 × 39.4 cm)
- Embroidery floss: 1 skein each of ecru, black, purple, and dark purple
- Pillow stuffing

Stitches

Back Stitch, Straight Stitch, Split Stitch, Satin Stitch, Hidden Stitch

109

Instructions

1   Using ¼ inch (6 mm) seams, sew each set of three patterned blocks together along the long sides to make the top and bottom panels of the front of the pillow.

2   Next, sew the lavender piece in the middle to the top and bottom panels to form the pillow's front panel. Press the seams flat.

3   The panda motif should be the same size as shown on page 111. Transfer the panda and 2 flower motifs to the center panel. Arrange as shown in the photo below. Fabric pens bleed easily on satin, so I used the tissue paper method described on page 8.

4   Embroider the panda according to the pattern using all 6 threads of floss.

5   Now sew the front and back panels together, right sides facing together, leaving 4 inches (10.2 cm) open at the side.

6   Stuff the pillow firmly, and stitch up the hole using Hidden Stitch.

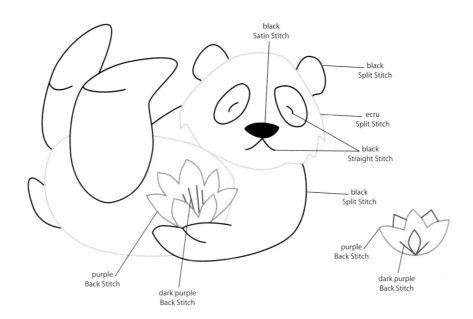

black
Satin Stitch

black
Split Stitch

ecru
Split Stitch

black
Straight Stitch

black
Split Stitch

purple
Back Stitch

purple
Back Stitch

dark purple
Back Stitch

dark purple
Back Stitch

Queen Bee Mini Quilt

PROJECT DESIGNER

AIMEE RAY

"Ticker tape" appliqué quilts are fun and easy. Fabric scraps made into "ticker tape" confetti is a great way to use up your leftovers.

What You Need

Templates: ticker tape pieces (page 160)

Embroidery design motifs: 4 small bees and 1 large bee; 4 honeycombs; honey pot; beehive; honey ladle; word (page 117)

3–5 different yellow and light brown patterned fabrics

Embroidery floss: 1 skein each of yellow, light yellow, dark brown, brown, light brown, and light green

1 square white or off-white fabric, 12 × 12 inches (30.5 × 30.5 cm), for the front

1 square yellow patterned fabric, 12 × 12 inches (30.5 × 30.5 cm), for the back

1 square quilt batting, 12 × 12 inches (30.5 × 30.5 cm)

Light yellow ½-inch-wide (1.3 cm) bias tape, 2 yards

Stitches

Back Stitch, Satin Stitch, Long and Short Stitch, Whip Stitch

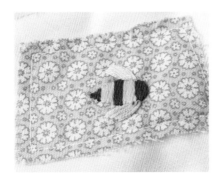

Instructions

1 Size the ticker tape pieces as indicated on page 160. Then transfer the designs onto the colored fabrics.

2 Transfer the embroidery design motifs onto the fabric ticker tape pieces. The designs should be the same size as shown on page 117.

3 Embroider the designs according to the patterns, using 3 of the 6 threads of floss.

4 Cut out the pieces, leaving the edges unfinished.

5 Arrange them on the white square as shown in the photo on page 112. Pin them in place.

NOTE: *You can now either quilt the three layers of your quilt together as you machine-sew the appliqué pieces in place, or you can tie the quilt by hand after sewing the pieces onto the front panel.*

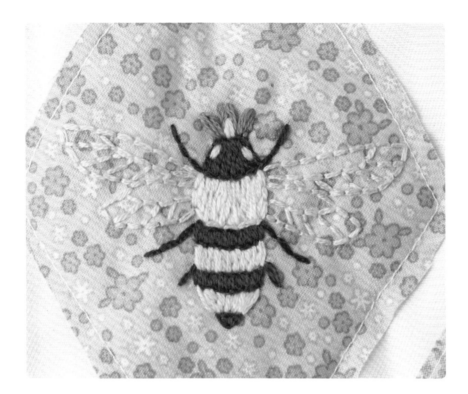

TO MACHINE-QUILT THE PROJECT IN ONE STEP

1   Line up the top square, batting, and bottom square, and pin them together.

2   Sew around the edge of each ticker tape piece ¼ inch (6.35 mm) from the edge, through all three layers.

TO TIE THE QUILT BY HAND

1   Sew the appliqué pieces onto the front panel.

2   Pin the three layers together.

3   To make the ties, thread a needle with white floss and pass it through all the layers from back to front, then front to back, making a small stitch. Tie the floss in a tight double knot, and trim the ends to ½ inch (1.3 cm). Make ties about 2 inches (5.1 cm) apart with the knots at the back. Hide the stitches on the front under the edges of the appliqué pieces.

TO FINISH THE QUILT

1. Cut 4 pieces of bias tape 14 inches (35.6 cm) long, one for each edge.

2. Sew the bias tape onto the edges of the quilt, centering the quilt on the strip of bias tape. Unfold a length of bias tape and line it up with one raw edge of the quilt top, right sides facing together. Pin the binding in place, and stitch along the fold nearest the edge. Trim off the extra batting and backing so that the quilt edge is even with the edge of the binding. Fold the binding over the edge of the quilt, and stitch it to the backing along the other folded edge using the Appliqué Stitch. Stop stitching 1 inch (2.5 cm) short of the edges of the quilt. Attach a piece of binding to the other three edges in the same way.

3. To make a corner, trim off one end of the binding so that it lines up with the edge of the quilt. Fold the other raw end of binding under itself, and wrap it over the raw corner to the back, lining it up with the edge of the quilt. Hand-sew the end closed using Whip Stitch. Continue stitching each corner closed in the same way.

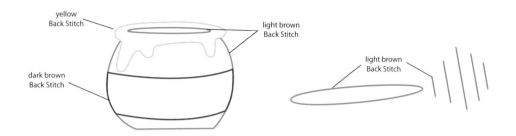

yellow
Back Stitch

light brown
Back Stitch

dark brown
Back Stitch

light brown
Back Stitch

yellow
Back Stitch

HONEY

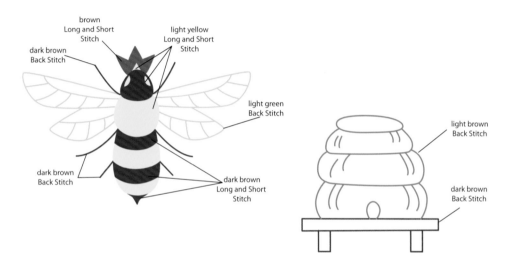

brown
Long and Short
Stitch

light yellow
Long and Short
Stitch

dark brown
Back Stitch

light green
Back Stitch

dark brown
Back Stitch

dark brown
Long and Short
Stitch

light brown
Back Stitch

dark brown
Back Stitch

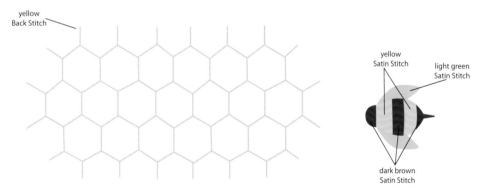

yellow
Back Stitch

yellow
Satin Stitch

light green
Satin Stitch

dark brown
Satin Stitch

117

Scallop Banner

PROJECT DESIGNER

Aimee Ray

Banners are one of my favorite decorations. I have different styles all over my house, and I leave many of them up year-round. This banner reminds me of a cute vintage kitchen, but it is perfect for brightening up any room.

What You Need

Templates: 7-inch (17.8 cm) circle; 6-inch (15.2 cm) circle (page 161)

13 pieces red, blue, aqua, and pink fabrics in different patterns, 7 × 7 inches (17.8 × 17.8 cm)

Pinking shears

Iron

Pins

Carbon paper or tissue paper

Embroidery design motifs (page 121)

Embroidery floss: 1 skein each of red, aqua, blue, and pink

Piece of grosgrain ribbon, 8 feet (2.4 cm) long × 1 inch (2.5 cm) wide

Stitches

Running Stitch, Back Stitch, French Knot, Lazy Daisy Stitch, Satin Stitch

Instructions

1 Use the circle templates and pinking shears to cut out 4 circles 7 inches (17.8 cm) in diameter and 9 circles 6 inches (15.2 cm) in diameter.

2 Center one small circle on top of each larger one to create a double circle layer, and press them all flat.

3 Pin the small circles in place on the larger ones, and stitch them on using Running Stitch.

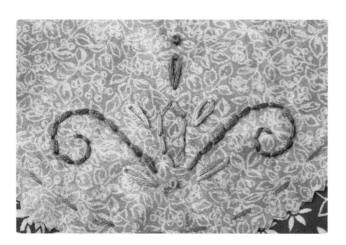 

4   Now fold each circle or pair of circles in half, and press them flat again.

5   Using either the carbon paper or the tissue paper method, transfer one of the embroidery patterns onto one side of each of the larger double circles. The designs should be the same size as shown on page 121.

6   Stitch them according to the pattern using all 6 threads of floss.

7   Using 2 threads of embroidery floss matching the fabrics, stitch each half-circle closed ½ inch (1.3 cm) from the edge using Running Stitch. Leave the top 1 inch (2.5 cm) open next to the fold on both sides.

8   Slide the ribbon through the openings at the top of each half-circle, alternating large and small. Make two small stitches on the back of each half-circle, attaching them to the ribbon.

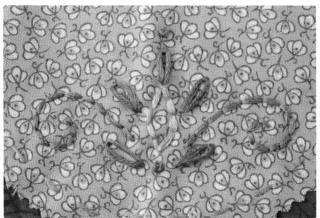

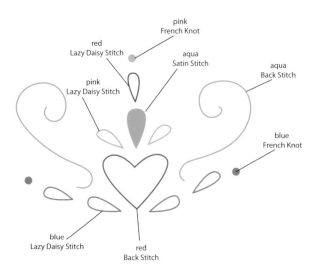

pink
French Knot

red
Lazy Daisy Stitch

aqua
Satin Stitch

pink
Lazy Daisy Stitch

aqua
Back Stitch

blue
French Knot

blue
Lazy Daisy Stitch

red
Back Stitch

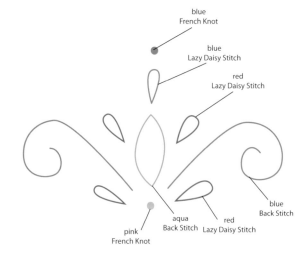

blue
French Knot

blue
Lazy Daisy Stitch

red
Lazy Daisy Stitch

blue
Back Stitch

pink
French Knot

aqua
Back Stitch

red
Lazy Daisy Stitch

Simple Squares
Reversible Wrap Skirt

PROJECT DESIGNER

AIMEE RAY

This skirt is super simple, super cute, and wearable all year round.

What You Need

This project uses a ½-inch (1.3 cm) seam allowance throughout.

60 pieces fabric in spring colors, 5 inches (12.7 cm) square

60 pieces fabric in fall colors, 5 inches (12.7 cm) square

2 pieces fabric in light green, 21 × 4 inches (53.3 × 10.2 cm)

2 pieces fabric in dark green, 21 × 4 inches (53.3 × 10.2 cm)

1 piece fabric in light green (pieced together is fine), 53 × 5½ inches (134.6 × 14.0 cm)

1 piece fabric in dark green (pieced together is fine), 53 × 5½ inches (134.6 × 14.0 cm)

Carbon paper

Embroidery design motif (page 125)

Embroidery floss: one skein each of dark green and light green

Pins

Stitches

Back Stitch, Straight Stitch, Satin Stitch, Topstitch, Hidden Stitch

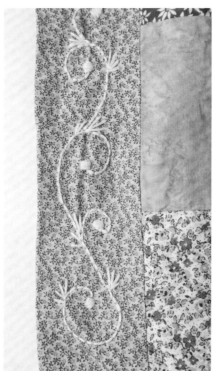

Instructions

1. Sew the spring color blocks together into a 5 × 12-block panel (to change the size, see the Tip on the facing page).

2. Do the same with the fall colors.

3. Use one panel to wrap around your waist and measure the size.

   NOTE: *This size will usually fit, but if you need to add or remove a row or two for a different size, make that adjustment now. You'll want the ends to overlap in front at least one square's width before adding the edge pieces.*

4. Sew the light green 21 × 4-inch (53.3 × 10.2 cm) pieces to either end of the spring panel.

5. Repeat with the fall fabric pieces, sewing the dark green pieces to the fall panel.

6. For the skirt ties, fold each 53 × 5½-inch (134.6 × 14.0 cm) strip in half lengthwise with right sides facing together, and sew up the edge using a ½-inch (1.3 cm) seam allowance. Taper 1 end to a point. Leave the other end open. Turn each strip right side out and press the seams flat.

7. Using the carbon paper, transfer the embroidery pattern to one of the dark green sides and one of the light green sides near the bottom edge. The design should be the same size as shown on page 125.

8. Embroider the dark fabric with light green floss and the light fabric with dark green floss using all 6 threads of floss.

9. Lay out the front and back skirt panels with right sides facing, and pin them together. Tuck one of the ties inside (between the two panels) on each side at the top of the skirt. Position the open end of the tie so that it is aligned along the outside edge and will be sewn into the side seam.

10. Sew around the entire skirt, leaving a 4-inch (10.2 cm) opening along the top edge for turning, being careful not to catch the loose ties in the seams.

11. Turn the skirt right side out and press. Top Stitch along the top edge of the skirt, and stitch the turning hole closed using Hidden Stitch.

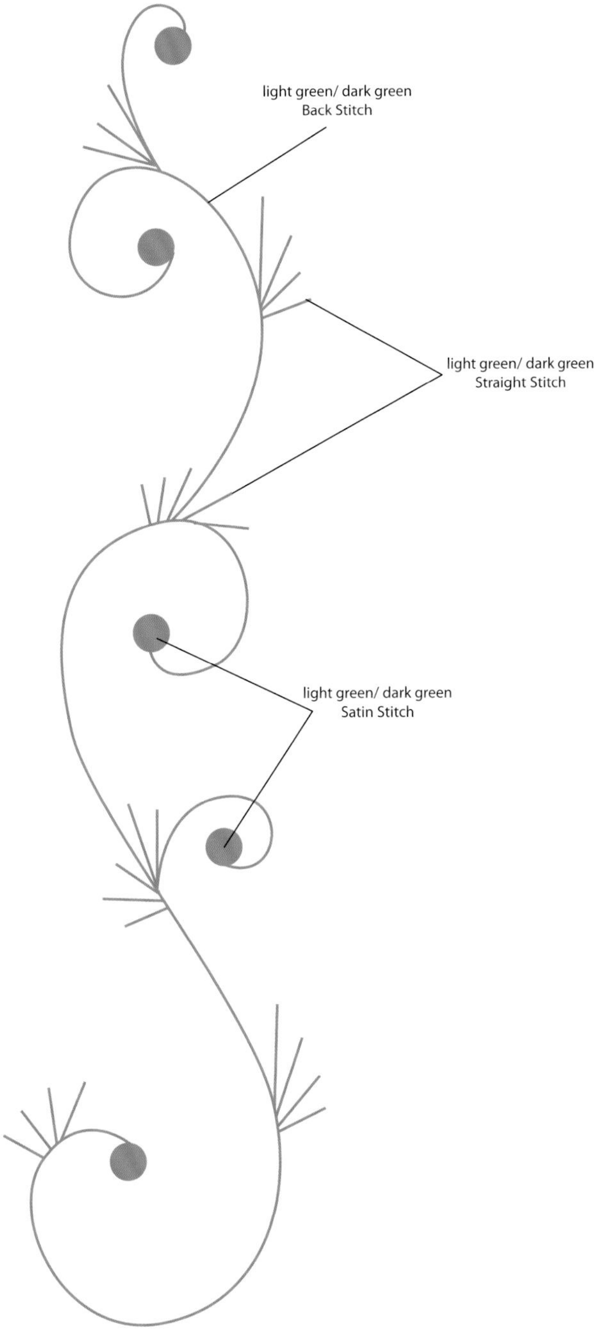
light green/ dark green
Back Stitch
light green/ dark green
Straight Stitch
light green/ dark green
Satin Stitch

TIP

You can approximate in advance how many blocks are necessary to fit you properly by measuring around your hips with a tape measure. Add 4 inches (10.2 cm) to that number for the overlap, and then divide by 4 (10.2) (the size of each block). This is approximately the number of blocks you will need to go around you. If you get a fraction of a block, round up to the next full number.

You can also approximate the desired length of your skirt by measuring from your waist to your knee (or wherever you would like the skirt to be hemmed). Take this number and divide by 4 (10.2) to get the number of blocks for the second dimension of the block panels you will be sewing.

Sweet Strawberry Blossom Phone Pouch

PROJECT DESIGNER

MOLLIE JOHANSON

Keep your phone safe and extra cute with this easy pouch. The patchwork is pieced by hand using English paper piecing with only a bit of machine sewing, so you can make and use your phone case on the go!

What You Need

Carbon paper

Embroidery design motif: strawberry blossom (page 128)

1 piece linen in taupe, 4 × 4 inches (10.2 × 10.2 cm)

3-inch embroidery hoop

Embroidery floss: red, very light avocado green, medium yellow, and white

Template: 16 hexagon templates, 1 inch (2.5 cm) (page 152)

1 sheet plain copier paper

Washable glue stick

15 fabric scraps in shades and patterns of red, at least 2½ inches (6.8 cm) square

Needle and thread

Pins

1 piece felt in red, 6½ × 5¼ inches (16.5 × 13.3 cm)

6 inches elastic cording

1 red button

Stitches

Back Stitch, Basting Stitch, Whip Stitch, Running Stitch

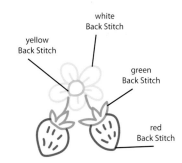

yellow
Back Stitch

white
Back Stitch

green
Back Stitch

red
Back Stitch

TIPS

Because phone sizes vary, you may need to adjust the size of the pouch by adding an extra row of hexagons to the top or bottom.

Add an extra row of hexagons to the bottom to make this case into a pouch for your sunglasses!

Instructions

1   Using the carbon paper, transfer the strawberry blossom design onto the linen. The design should be the same size as shown at left.

2   Place the fabric in the hoop and embroider the design. Use 3 strands of floss, and Back Stitch throughout.

3   Remove all the markings.

4   Trace the hexagon template (page 152) onto the copier paper 16 times, and cut out the shapes. Take care to make certain that all templates are exactly the same.

5   Use a washable glue stick to adhere a hexagon template to the back of the embroidery, taking care to center it.

6   Attach the remaining hexagon templates to the backs of the red fabrics.

7   Cut around each template, leaving a ⅜-inch (9.5 mm) seam allowance.

8   Select the first hexagon and, with the paper template secured to the fabric, start along 1 edge. Fold the fabric carefully up and over the paper, creating a straight folded edge.

9   While holding the first folded edge in place, move to an adjacent side and fold it up and over the paper as well.

10 Using a standard sewing needle and thread and Basting Stitch, baste the fabric only at the corner to hold it in place. Take care not to sew the fabric to the paper.

11 Repeat this folding and basting along each edge of the hexagon until all sides have been folded over the paper edges and secured with the basting thread.

   NOTE: *Create straight folds and crisp corners to ensure that your hexagons fit together perfectly.*

12 Repeat the basting process for each hexagon.

13 Using Whip Stitch, join the hexagons in 4 rows of 4 hexagons each. Viewing the layout of the 4-by-4 block panel face up, position the embroidered hexagon in the third row from the top and in the second place from the left.

14 Fold the panel in half, right sides together, and join the hexagons to form a tube.

15 Remove the paper templates and lay the tube so that the embroidered hexagon is centered horizontally. Trim the points from the bottom edge, pin, and sew straight across with a ¼-inch (6 mm) seam allowance.

16 Turn the pouch right side out.

17 Fold the felt in half, forming a 3¼ × 5¼-inch (8.3 × 13.3 cm) rectangle. Sew the long edge and one short edge. Nestle the felt pouch inside the pieced pouch.

18 Fold in the points at the top of the pouch and pin to the felt lining.

19 Tie a double knot in each end of the elastic cording. Position the elastic between the exterior and lining, with one end at each side of the back center hexagon.

20 Stitch around the top of the pouch with three strands of red embroidery floss. Use a small Running Stitch, and make sure you catch the knots in the elastic. Take an extra stitch through each elastic knot to make it secure.

21 Sew the button on the front of the pouch at the bottom of the center hexagon.

Tic-Tac-Toe Board

PROJECT DESIGNER

TERESA MAIRAL BARREU

The board is a 9-patch block with sashing. The finished board is about 10¾ inches (27.3 cm) square.

What You Need

FOR THE GAME BOARD

5 squares red fabric, 4 × 4 inches (10.2 × 10.2 cm)

4 squares contrasting fabric, 4 × 4 inches (10.2 × 10.2 cm)

4 strips of a different contrasting fabric, 10½ inches × 1 inch (26.7 × 2.5 cm)

1 square fabric for backing, 11 × 11 inches (27.9 × 27.9 cm)

1 square quilt batting, 11 × 11 inches (27.9 × 27.9 cm)

1 strip of contrasting fabric for edge binding (or the same amount of purchased bias tape), 2 × 45 inches (5.1 × 114.3 cm)

FOR THE TOKENS

Template: square, 3 inches (7.6 cm) (page 162)

1 square fabric in white for the embroidered sides, 13 × 13 inches (33.0 × 33.0 cm)

Carbon paper

Embroidery design motifs: circles, crosses (page 133)

9 squares of fabric for the bottom of the cushions, 4 in one fabric and 5 in another, 3 × 3 inches (7.6 × 7.6 cm)

6 strips of fabric, 1 × 3 inches (2.5 cm × 7.6 cm) each

2 strips of fabric, 10½ inches × 1 inch (26.7 × 2.5 cm) each

Embroidery floss: 1 skein each in red and black

Fiber filler

Stitches

Running Stitch, Back Stitch for the outer crosses and circles, Slip Stitch, Hidden Stitch

Instructions

FOR THE GAME BOARD

1 Lay out fabric, alternating 1 red square, 1 white strip of fabric, 1 black square, 1 white strip of fabric, and one more red square, and sew together in that order. Make two rows this way (row 1 and 3 of the board)

2 For the middle row, alternate a black square, a white strip, a red square, and a white strip, and finish with a black square.

3 Press all seams open.

4 Sew one of the long strips of white fabric along row 1, and then sew row 2 on the other side of the white strip.

5 Now sew another long strip of white fabric on the other side of row 2.

6 Sew row 3 to the other side of the long strip of white fabric.

7 Press all seams open. This completes the board game patchwork top.

8 If necessary, trim the ends of the strips to be even with the edges of the patch.

9 Make a quilt sandwich by placing the backing fabric wrong side up on your work surface. Align the quilt batting over the backing fabric, and then place the patchwork piece, right side up, on top. Pin and quilt.

NOTE: *I machine-quilted using straight lines at ½-inch (1.3 cm) intervals.*

10 After quilting, trim excess batting and backing fabric.

11 Add the binding. Place the quilted patchwork right side up, and lay the raw edge of the strip of binding facedown along 1 edge and starting at 1 corner. Allow ½ inch (1.3 cm) of the binding to extend beyond the corner of the patch. The raw edge of the binding and the patchwork will be aligned.

12 Pin around the square, taking care to fold the binding evenly into a mitered corner at each turn. Use the overhanging binding at the starting corner to form a nice miter at the end. Sew the binding to the patch ¼ inch (6 mm) from the edge.

13 Wrap the binding around the edge of the patch onto the back side. Slip Stitch the folded edge of the binding to the back by hand.

FOR TOKENS

1 Trace the template square (page 162) on white fabric 9 times (4 circles and 5 crosses).

   NOTE: *It will be easy to separate the 9 squares later, if you butt the edges of squares together to make a grid. Then a few simple straight cuts will produce the smaller squares.*

2 Using the carbon paper, transfer 1 of the motifs onto each of the squares. Make 4 circles and 5 crosses. Each design should be the same size as shown below.

3 Embroider the designs.

4 Select the 5 embroidered crosses and the 5 pieces of coordinating backing fabric. Take one of each, and match them up right sides facing together. Sew around the edges using a ¼-inch (6 mm) seam allowance. Leave a 1-inch (2.5 cm) opening to turn right side out.

5 Turn the tokens right side out, and lightly fill with fiber filler.

6 Stitch the opening closed using an invisible stitch, such as the Hidden Stitch.

7 Repeat with the 4 embroidered circles and the 4 pieces of coordinating backing fabric.

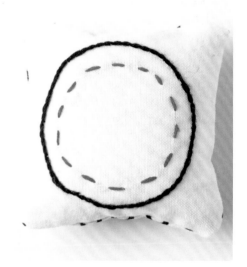

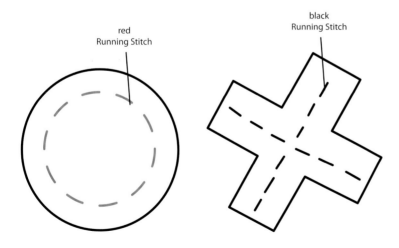

red
Running Stitch

black
Running Stitch

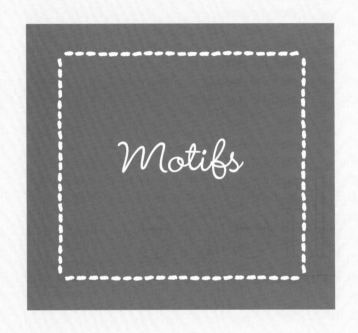

Motifs

Dream

wish

Believe

create

136

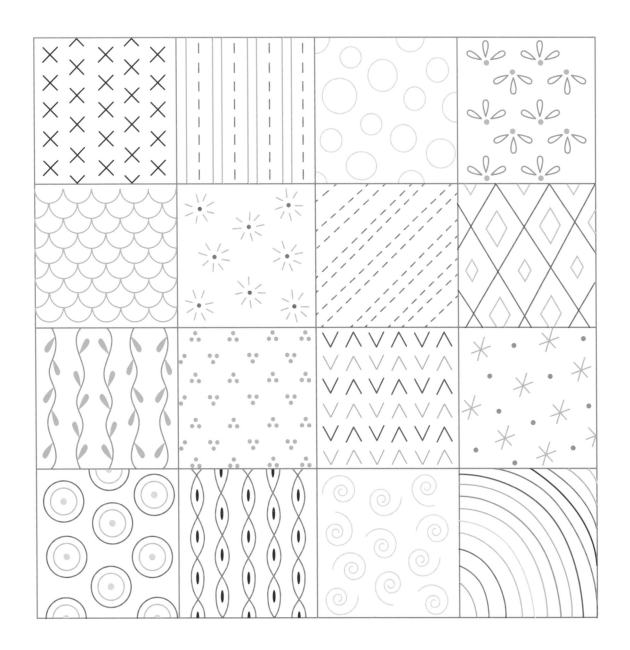

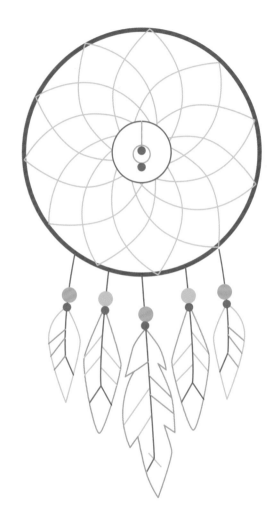

144

148

Templates

Sweet Strawberry Blossom
Phone Pouch

Page 127 – 100%

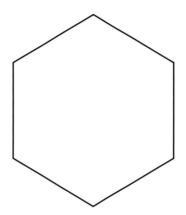

Camper Zipper Pouch

Page 39 – 100%

Lavendar Hexagon Sachet

Page 79 – 100%

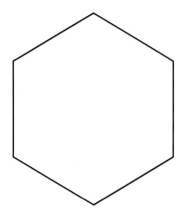

Hexagon Hanging Hoop

Page 57 – 100%

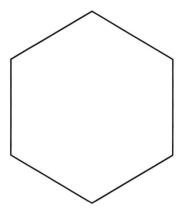

Journal Ruler

Enlarge 125%

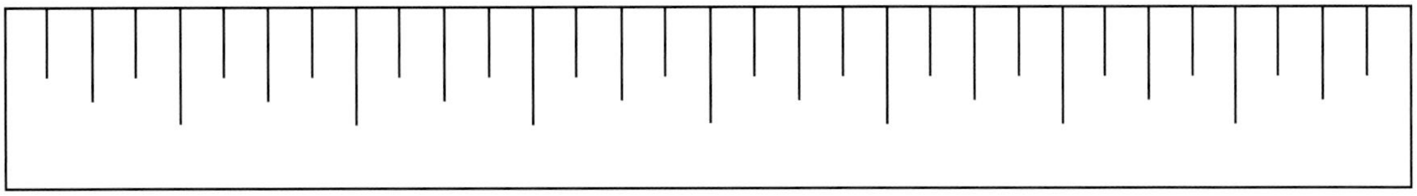

Journal Cover

Page 67

Enlarge 200%

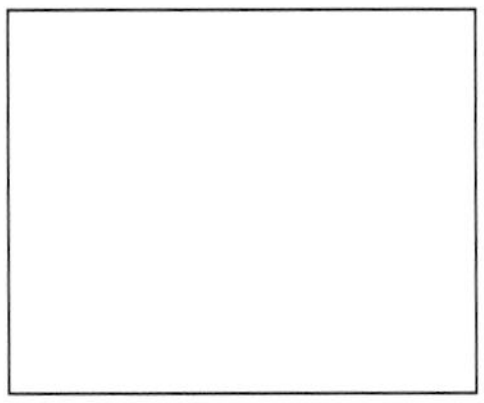

Enlarge 200%

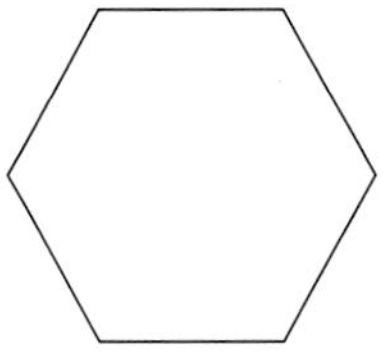

Enlarge 200%

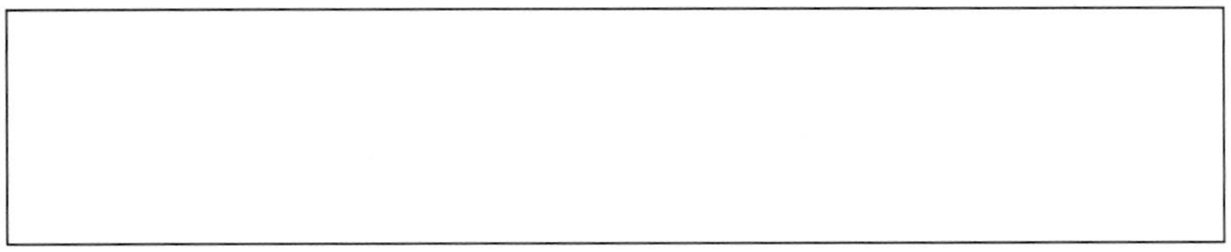

Enlarge 200%

Enlarge 250%

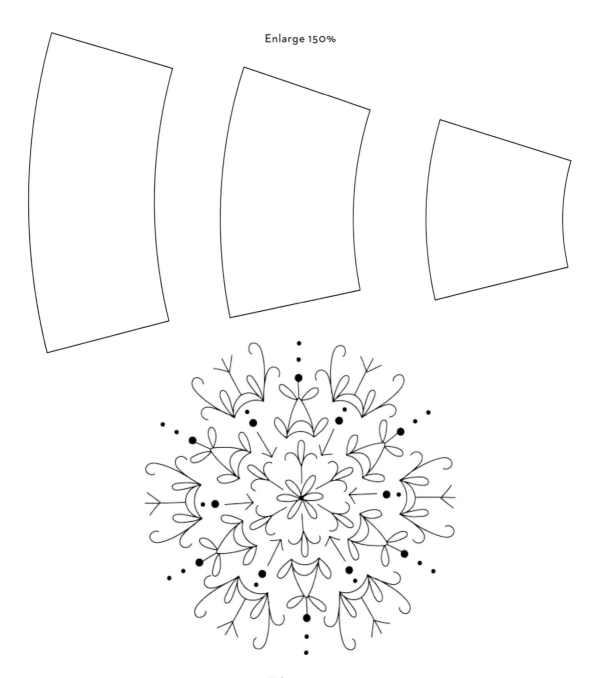

Enlarge 150%

Mushroom Pin Cushion

Page 95 – Enlarge 150%

158

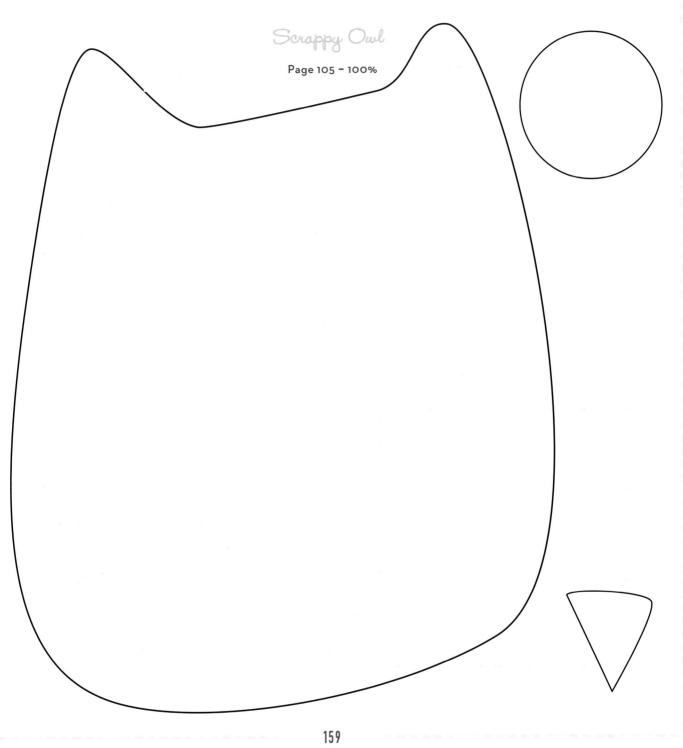

Scrappy Owl

Page 105 - 100%

Queen Bee Mini Quilt

Page 113 – Enlarge 175%

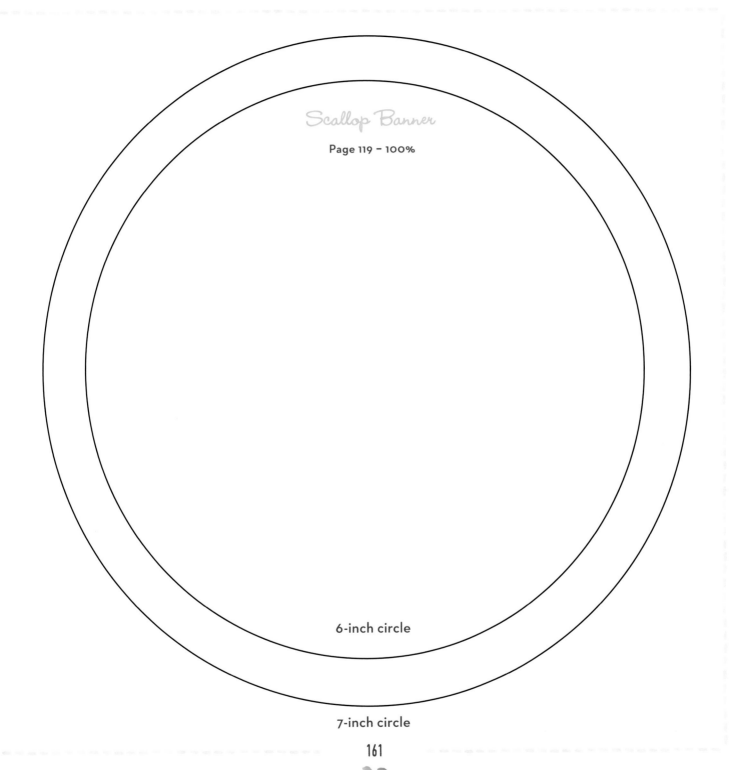

Scallop Banner

Page 119 – 100%

6-inch circle

7-inch circle

Page 131 – 100%

3-inch square

About the Designers

ANNIE KIGHT

Armed with a glue gun at a young age, Annie took her glittering very seriously. After many moons in the confectionery world, she opted in for the life of a mini-sculptress. She daydreams a lot and rarely sleeps, which makes for a pie-in-the-sky kind of existence. You can find her pincushions, polymer clay pin toppers, and dollhouse miniatures at etsy.com/shop/PinksAndNeedles, and keep up with her at her blog, pinksandneedles.blogspot.com.

TERESA MAIRAL BARREU

Born and raised in Spain, Teresa learned knitting, crochet, and embroidery from her sewer, knitter, and lace-making mother. After moving to Australia as an adult and a long craftless spell, she caught the crafting bug again and became interested in patchwork and fabric. Now living in Paris, she spends her spare time sewing and designing. When she's not sewing, Teresa can be found drawing, painting, sculpting, embroidering, or felting. Her blog, *Sewn Up by TheresaDownUnder*, can be found at mypatchwork.wordpress.com.

CARINA ENVOLDSEN-HARRIS

Carina Envoldsen-Harris is a designer, blogger, and author. Originally from Denmark, she now lives just outside London with her English husband. Carina has been making things for as long as she can remember—painting, drawing, and embroidering. Under the name Polka & Bloom, she creates colorful patterns and fabric designs. You can see more of her work in her book, *Stitched Blooms* (Lark Crafts, 2013), and on her blog, carinascraftblog.com.

MOLLIE JOHANSON

Mollie Johanson, the author of *Stitch Love: Sweet Creatures Big & Small* from Lark Crafts (2015), has loved cute things, creative messes, and cuddly critters for as long as she can remember. Her blog at www.wildolive.blogspot.com is known for embroidery patterns, simply stitched projects, and playful printables, most often presenting charming creations with smiling faces. Her work has been featured on *Mollie Makes, Australian Homespun,* and in a variety of books, including several Lark Crafts titles.

CYNTHIA SHAFFER

Cynthia Shaffer is a mixed media artist, creative sewer, and photographer whose love of sewing can be traced back to childhood. She is the author of *Stash Happy Patchwork* (Lark Crafts, 2011), *Stash Happy Appliqué* (Lark Crafts, 2012), *Coastal Crafts* (Lark Crafts, 2015), *Simply Stitched Gifts* (Lark Crafts, 2015), and coauthor of *Serge It* (Lark Crafts, 2014). In her spare time Cynthia knits, crochets, paints, and dabbles in all sorts of crafts. Cynthia lives with her husband, Scott, sons Corry and Cameron, and beloved dogs Harper and Berklee in Southern California. For more information, visit Cynthia online at cynthiashaffer.typepad.com or www.cynthiashaffer.com.

About the Author

Aimee Ray has been an artist all her life. She loves all types of art and crafts and is always trying something new. Besides embroidery, she dabbles in illustration, watercolor, miniature sculpting, crochet, weaving, and doll-making. Aimee lives in northwest Arkansas with her husband, Josh, and their son and daughter.

Aimee has written four previous books of contemporary embroidery designs: *Doodle Stitching* (Lark Crafts, 2007); *Doodle Stitching: The Motif Collection* (Lark Crafts, 2010); *Doodle Stitching: Embroidery & Beyond* (Lark Crafts, 2013); *Doodle Stitching: The Holiday Motif Collection* (Lark Crafts, 2014). She is also the author of *Aimee Ray's Sweet & Simple Jewelry* (Lark Crafts, 2013). She has also contributed to many other Lark Craft titles and sells even more original embroidery and craft patterns at her Etsy shop. You can see more of her work at www.aimeeray.com and follow her daily crafting endeavors at www.littledeartracks.blogspot.com.

Acknowledgments

I hope you enjoy Patchwork Embroidery *as much as we enjoyed working on it!* Big thanks go to my husband, Josh, and my family, who always encourage me in everything I do. My mom, grandmas, and creative aunties were always making something when I was growing up and instilled in me a love of crafting. I owe lots of inspiration to them. And big thank-yous to all the fabulous designers who created so many of the projects in this book! Be sure and follow the links in each of their profiles and "oooh and aaah" over what they do in their own crafty worlds.

Index

Note: Page numbers in italics indicate templates.